D0131435

Art Center College of Design
Library
1700 Lida Street
Pasadena, Calif. 91103

Art Center College of Design
Library
1700 Lida Street
Pasadena, Calif. 91103

ART CENTER COLLEGE OF DESIGN

3 3220 00206 6749

PATTERNS

OF

PROGRESS

746.46074
B797
1997

PATTERNS OF PROGRESS

QUILTS IN THE

MACHINE AGE

Barbara Brackman

Art Center College of Design
Library
1700 Lida Street
Pasadena, Calif. 91103

Autry Museum of Western Heritage

Los Angeles, California

Copyright © 1997 by Autry Museum of Western Heritage.
4700 Western Heritage Way, Los Angeles, CA 90027-1462.
All rights reserved.

This project has been supported through the generosity of the
Glendale Quilt Guild and The Textile Group of Los Angeles.

Library of Congress Cataloging-in-Publication Data

Brackman, Barbara.
    Patterns of progress: quilts in the machine age/Barbara Brackman.
    p. cm.
    Exhibition catalog.
    Includes bibliographical references.
    ISBN 1-882880-03-X. — ISBN 1-882880-04-8 (pbk.)
    1. Machine quilting—West (U.S.)—History—19th century—Exhibitions.
    2. Machine quilting—West (U.S.)—History—20th century—Exhibitions.
    3. Quilts—West (U.S.)—History—19th century—Exhibitions.
    4. Quilts—West (U.S.)—History—20th century—Exhibitions.
    5. Quiltmakers—West (U.S.)—History—19th century—Exhibitions.
    6. Quiltmakers—West (U.S.)—History—20th century—Exhibitions.
    I. Autry Museum of Western Heritage. II. Title.
    TT835.B6422   1997
    746.46'074794'94—dc21   97-13375
                                       CIP

Manufactured in China.

Book Production Manager: Suzanne G. Fox

Designer: Jon Cournoyer

Photo credits:

Cover: *Oak Leaves* (detail), made by Mabry Benson, Kensington, California, 1997.
           78 x 82 inches. Machine-pieced, machine-appliquéd and machine-quilted. Collection of the maker.

Page 2:   *The Paper Pieced Sun* (detail), made by Marie Fritz, San Diego, California, 1997.
           88 x 88 inches. Machine-pieced, hand-quilted. Collection of the maker.

Page 5:   *Journey II* (detail), made by Erika Carter, Bellevue, Washington, 1995. 50 x 46 inches.
           Hand-painted, machine-appliquéd and machine-quilted. Collection of the maker.

Page 6:   *Nate Love African American Cowboy* (detail), made by Carolyn Mazloomi, Cincinnati, Ohio, 1996.
           60 x 72 inches. Hand- and machine-appliquéd and machine-quilted. Collection of the maker.

Except for the following images, all photographs in this book were taken by Susan Einstein, Los Angeles, California.
All images are listed by plate or figure numbers.

Caryl Bryer Fallert: Plates 55 and 56.
Harriett Hargrave: Plates 51 and 52.
Barbara and Kern Jackson: Plates 17 and 18.
Kansas Collection, University of Kansas Libraries, Lawrence, Kansas: Figure 5.
Kansas Quilt Project, Inc.: Figure 12.
Kansas State Historical Society, Topeka, Kansas: Figures 1, 11; Plate 20.
Libby Lehman: Plate 63.
Montana Historical Society Photograph Archives, Helena, Montana: Figure 4.
Nebraska State Historical Society, Lincoln, Nebraska: Figure 3.
Oakland Museum of California, Oakland, California: Plate 16.
Private collection: Plates 1, 2, 4, 10, 13; Figures 2, 6, 7, 8, 9, 10, 13.
Terry Clothier Thompson, Lawrence, Kansas: Plate 12.

FOREWORD

The Autry Museum of Western Heritage is committed to sharing the stories of all the peoples and cultures that have been part of the American West. Through exhibitions, publications, lectures and other programs, we have explored topics ranging from the story of Russian settlements in America, to the history of Japanese American women, to the roots of Western music. The Autry Museum continues to challenge people's notions of what the American West is. We go far beyond cowboys and Indians.

Following the success of a traveling exhibition of quilts from the 1933 Chicago World's Fair, we have actively worked to develop an exhibition that situates quilts within the culture of the West. In such a context, quilts become more than just bed coverings: they are cultural artifacts, revealing much about women's lives, their roles and perceptions of the world.

Patterns of Progress: Quilts in the Machine Age is an examination of quilts as clues to the lives of women, especially those who lived and worked in the West, and to the changes they experienced because of the invention and accessibility of the sewing machine. We thank Barbara Brackman, the guest curator, for her proposal and hard work on the catalogue and the exhibition. Her knowledge and enthusiasm have been phenomenal. Sandi Fox and Rebecca Hunt also have been a great help to this project. We are also grateful to the Glendale Quilt Guild, whose members have been wonderful supporters of the museum and its exhibitions.

The catalogue and the exhibition would not have been possible without the support of the many lenders; we owe them a very special thanks for their generosity and enthusiasm. Finally, I would like to acknowledge the contribution of Susan Einstein, whose wonderful photographs of the quilts in this catalogue will help us share them with a wider audience.

A special thanks goes to Joanne Hale, President and Chief Executive Officer of the Autry Museum of Western Heritage, for her unfailing enthusiasm. Many individuals from the collections management, curatorial, exhibitions, conservation, development, education, publications, facilities and security departments have cooperated to produce this project. Everything accomplished at the Autry is done through team efforts, which have fostered the many successes of the institution.

Through publications, the Autry Museum is expanding its educational mission, with the intent to widen understanding of the history of the American West and those who have participated in it. We hope that this book will continue that tradition, encouraging those who read it to consider ideas that often have been overlooked.

Theresa R. González
Project Manager,
Patterns of Progress,
and Assistant Curator

FIGURE 1.
Women in this class in Osborne, Kansas, in 1899, do
both plain and fancy sewing by hand. Plain sewing
included making clothing and household linens;
fancy work was decorative. Courtesy of the Kansas
State Historical Society, Topeka, Kansas.

Patterns Of Progress
Quilts In The Machine Age

Barbara Brackman

"I have been busy, so busy, I could not write you. But now I can. I have sewed so much that I have cut my fingers bad with the thread. I cannot sew so steady." [1]

PLATE 1.

Detail of an appliqué sampler, made by a member of the Fitzsimmons family, possibly in Jacksonville, Illinois, 1840–1865. Hand-appliquéd and hand-quilted. Collection of Barbara and Kern Jackson, Arkansas. Such fine handwork skills as stuffed quilting and buttonhole appliqué were forgotten as the sewing machine changed women's lives in the last half of the nineteenth century.

Today sewing is often recreation. Freed from having to produce clothing at home by the cheapness of factory-made garments, many look forward to a day spent at the sewing machine. The life of the nineteenth-century housewife was so different that it often is difficult to imagine, but Georgia Whitwell's words give a glimpse of the day-in, day-out drudgery they faced with their needles.

Needlework, either plain or fancy, was women's work. Plain sewing was the production of clothing and linens for the household, the task for which girls were trained from childhood, the task that occupied women throughout their lives. Fancy sewing, the decorative arts such as embroidery and appliqué, filled women's leisure hours.

Women not only sewed to keep their families clothed; many also relied on their needle skills to keep their children fed. A Mrs. Gregson remembered the days in the California mining country, when her husband was earning a dollar a day. "We women folk took in all the sewing such as making overalls. We could make $10 per day in Sonoma . . . I took in washing and ironing and sewing to support my family . . . . I would sew until 1 or 2 o'clock in the night and in the day I would wash and take care of the babes." [2]

Plate 2.
Stereocard from Underwood and
Underwood, Ottawa, Kansas,
1898. Private collection.
Before the advent of the
machine, girls as young as four
or five years old were taught to
sew patchwork. Piecing quilts
was considered excellent training
for a life of hand sewing. Even at
the end of the century, young
girls still stitched a stint of patchwork everyday, although it is
apparent that precision was not a
part of this girl's curriculum in
the machine age.

Aware of the tediousness and inefficiency of hand sewing, inventors had long searched for a way to mechanize the task. They first tried to imitate the hand stitch, the in-and-out motion of human fingers forcing a needle through layers of cloth. Machinery could not efficiently sew in human fashion, so success lay in thinking of new ways to run thread through fabric. The first recorded patent for a practical machine was awarded to an Englishman in 1790, but Thomas Saint never manufactured his machine for "stitching, quilting or sewing."

In 1829 Barthlemy Thimonnier patented a functional machine in France. Within a dozen years he had eighty treadle machines efficiently stitching uniforms for the French Army. Fearful for their economic futures, a mob of angry tailors broke into the factory and destroyed Thimonnier's machines. He rebuilt, only to lose the new machines during the revolution of 1848 to another gang terrified of change. Thimonnier set out for America where innovation was valued more than tradition, but he arrived too late to be a significant player in the American market.

Walter Hunt is credited with making the first practical American machine. His 1834 model featured a needle with an eye at the point. Another innovation was the interlocked stitch, locking two threads into a continuous seam. The story is told that Hunt's daughter, who realized the potential of

FIGURE 2.
Unknown family, about 1865. Private collection.
No matter what her class and financial status, the woman of the home oversaw the manufacture of the household clothing from underwear to outerwear. This young mother may have used a sewing machine for the trim on her own bodice and hoop skirt, but typically most of the seams in this era were hand-stitched. The practice of showing off the machine stitching in the decorative trim while hiding the hand sewing is also evident in quilts of the time.

PLATE 3.

Trade Card. Private collection.

With a pun on the company name, the New Home factory captures the myth of Western migration.

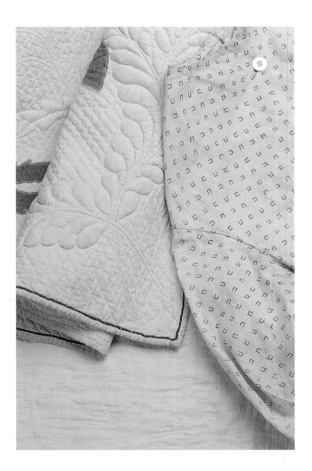

PLATE 4.

Detail of dress and quilt. Private collection.

Both dress and quilt date from the mid-nineteenth century, when a fine seam was the mark of a competent and educated woman. Decorative details in quilts reflected clothing construction and trim. The piping in the edge of the quilt also was commonly used for inserting sleeves. Once the sewing machine proliferated, seamstresses no longer added this corded detail.

a sewing machine, worried that it would deprive women seamstresses of their only livelihood. The altruistic Hunt abandoned his invention.

Ten years later, Elias Howe, Jr. re-invented Hunt's double-threaded machine with the eye at the needle's point, an innovation said to have appeared to him in a dream, and patented it in 1846. Unable to figure out a way to market the machine, Howe sailed for England, hoping for a better business climate. Failing there, he returned to America to find that in his absence several companies had infringed on his patents, manufacturing and selling a variety of machines with eye-pointed needles. Among the hardiest were the Wheeler and Wilson Company, and Isaac Singer. Howe sued all the manufacturers for royalties, demanding $25 for each machine sold. (This is one reason why early machines cost about $100 when average family income was only $500 a year.) Prices decreased when the patent wars were settled by manufacturers pooling the patents. Howe certainly benefited from his invention; at one point he went back to court complaining he had made only $1,185,000 in royalties.

The early machines manufactured from 1850 to 1856 were industrial machines, although some individuals bought them for home use. Singer's 1851 Number 1 machine, also called the "Jenny Lind," was a lock-stitch machine, much like present-day machines with one spool of thread above and a shuttle, rather than a bobbin, below. Other early machines were cranked with wheels requiring the use of one hand. In 1859 Singer and his unsung partner Edward Clark began manufacturing the Transverse Shuttle Letter A, a light "family" machine for the home market. Clark's most important contribution to the modern era was the installment plan. He realized that even a $75 machine was unaffordable, so he allowed families to pay it off at the rate of $5 per month. Singer and Clark did not invent the sewing machine, but they did invent monthly payments.

Eri B. Hulbert, one of Singer's early customers, recorded his encounter with the machine age in letters to his wife Louisa. He bought a machine

FIGURE 3.
The W.H. Blair family at Huckleberry, near Broken
Bow, Nebraska, 1888. Photograph by Solomon Butcher.
Courtesy of the Solomon D. Butcher Collection,
Nebraska State Historical Society, Lincoln, Nebraska.
A sod house might appear to have few luxuries, but the
Blairs boast clean clothing and a treadle machine.

directly from Isaac Singer in New York in 1852 as
he prepared to sail around the Horn to California
to make his fortune. He planned to spend the weeks
aboard ship stitching 1,000 bed ticks, which he
would sell in California to miners. He then intend-
ed to use the profits and the machine to go into the
leather and harness business. Singer had assured
him, "One fellow took one to California and wrote
he had made $20 a day with it ever since he had
been there, the only one who has gone there." [3]

Hulbert failed to talk Singer into a lower price
and paid the going rate of $125. After buying a life
insurance policy, he was short of cash to pay the
freight for his machine, so he abandoned the plan to
sail around the Horn. He packed the heavy machine
across the Isthmus, a fateful decision, because he
died of fever in Central America. His machine—
possibly California's second import—arrived in
Sacramento without him.

Eri Hulbert's 1852 purchase is the earliest docu-
mented personal reference to buying a machine.
Ann Lewis Hardeman of Mississippi mentions a
new machine in her journal: "October 22, 1854.
My bro[the]r received a sewing machine on the
18th (I believe) but does not know from whence it
came." Despite the machine's mysterious appearance, Ann, who was caring for her brother's moth-

erless children, settled down to use it. "November 5. Made two dresses for the little girls, sewed all the seams on the machine." [4]

Another early reference is in Mary Sharpe Jones's letter to her mother, who was living on the family plantation in Georgia and considering purchasing a machine. "December 27, 1856. One as Cousin Eliza has can be obtained for a hundred dollars, and for twenty more a box for covering and protecting the machine. I have not yet seen Cousin Eliza's in operation; as she has so much company with her at present, she has no time to prepare work for it." Mary's mother, another Mary Jones, replied in a day or two. "How much did Mrs. Gilmer's sewing machine cost? A hundred dollars is a great deal to invest in an uncertainty." [5]

Women's diaries and letters indicate that Southern women purchased machines earlier than Northern or Western women. It may be that the educated Southern women who kept journals tended, like the Joneses, to be upper class—slave holders responsible for supervising the clothing production for many people on plantations. The pre-Civil-War Southern home was more like a small factory, and the families had money to pay for machines.

The family that Rosina Klinger lived with in New York bought a machine in 1859. A recent German immigrant, Rosina wrote her father back in Wurttemberg: "Dear Father, we now have a sewing machine, but you mustn't think it's one like Aunt Katharina had, this is completely different, it cost 110 dollars, it sews all by itself you only have to pedal." Rosina did not reveal how her sister-in-law, another recent immigrant, could afford such a luxury. From her description, Aunt Katharina's German machine appears to have been powered by a hand crank, and the machine in New York had a foot-operated treadle. By the time Rosina's family machine arrived, treadles were becoming the standard, and American manufacturers tended to produce hand-cranked machines only for foreign markets. [6]

The Civil War in 1861 reduced sewing machine production, but the need for clothing, bedding and boots increased the use of machines in factories and homes. Sarah Jane Full Hill of St. Louis recalled that in 1861 "every loyal household became a soldiers' aid society . . . . We immediately set to work and made the sewing machine hum night and day. Mother, my aunt and we four older girls worked unceasingly and soon had a large box filled and ready to send to our soldier boys . . . . We made bed ticks which could be filled with hay or straw, could be easily emptied and refilled and took up but little room on a march. We made and tied comforters thick and warm . . . . and we made quantities of flannel shirts and kept the knitting needles clicking, fashioning socks and mittens. How the boys rejoiced over the contents of that box . . . . " Women north and south kept their machines humming. Raiders targeted sewing machines because soldiers knew a damaged machine could no longer supply the enemy. When Sarah Morgan's home in Baton Rouge was ransacked by Yankees who stole one of her machines, she wrote in her diary, "As Mother's was too heavy to move, they merely smashed the needles." [7]

Women in the West more typically purchased machines after the War. In 1871, Abbie Bright, a Kansas homesteader, was impressed enough by a new neighbor's possessions to list them in her diary: "nice bedding, nice linen table cloths and towels, etc., sheets—the nicest I have seen since I left home. She has a sewing machine too." Kansan Elise Dubach Iseley received a machine as an anniversary gift from her husband in 1873. In her memoirs she noted that the appearance of the sewing machine was a sign that "pioneer days were over." [8]

Women who had machines valued them highly. They were one of the few tangible possessions a woman might own. Having left her husband because "I didn't want no more children," Malinda Jenkins moved to Texas. She started over by opening a boarding house. In her memoirs, she recalled telling her landlord, "I ain't got but seven dollars and a half. I can't pay you nothing in advance. But I have a brand new Wheeler and Wilson sewing machine I'll put up till you get paid." Mrs. Conrad Sickles remembered the importance of her machine in Yakima County, Washington Territory, in the late 1870s. While new settlers and local tribes fought,

Plate 5.
Picture Puzzle: *Native Americans and the Singer,* 1906. Singer Sewing Machine Company. Autry Museum of Western Heritage. Advertisers often used Native Americans in their imagery, making the most of their exotic appeal. The image on the puzzle is derived from the photograph by N.A. Forsyth [Figure 4].

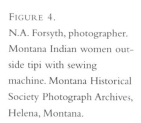

Figure 4.
N.A. Forsyth, photographer. Montana Indian women outside tipi with sewing machine. Montana Historical Society Photograph Archives, Helena, Montana.

FIGURE 5.
Indian Fair, Jackson County, Kansas, 1917. Jules A. Bourquin Collection, Kansas Collection,
University of Kansas Libraries, Lawrence, Kansas.
The Kickapoo and Potawatomie tribes held Indian Fairs from the turn of the century through the 1950s.
This display of entries under "Domestic and Fancy Work" includes blankets as well as quilts, indicating the range
of textiles in their repertoire. Sewing by hand and, later, by machine was a skill taught to native girls through-
out the mission system in the West.

PLATE 6.
Trade Card
Private Collection
Advertising campaigns featured cards that
appealed to collectors, with themes ranging
from foreign travel to sentiment to rustic
humor, as this card from the Domestic
Company shows.

her household was in a constant state of anxiety. "Our precious sewing machine was hidden in the cornfield at night for fear the Indians would come and burn the house." [9]

Machines came later to the West because of the problem of transportation, which added considerably to the price. Manufacturers have always been located in the Eastern states, especially Massachusetts and New York. Even by the 1900 census, there was only one manufacturer in the West, in Kansas. But as railroads facilitated freight and as mail-order shopping brought more Eastern goods to the frontier, machines became more available. Prices dropped in the 1870s, when patents expired and new companies sprang up to compete with more established manufacturers. [10]

Despite lower prices, better transportation and the installment plan, many working class and farming women entertained few hopes of buying machines. They did, however, have access to machine sewing through several types of cooperative ownership. The manufacturers cleverly donated machines to ministers' wives and other upstanding women, who then shared their machines. This marketing strategy was designed to give the sewing machine a certain cachet, and, most important, to prove that housewives could operate machinery—a concept that was not self-evident.

Through the last decades of the nineteenth-century women recorded other cooperative arrangements. Gertrude Nutter, a schoolteacher in Cuba, Kansas, borrowed a machine in 1896. "We have Mrs. Salley's sewing machine here this week and have made two sheets, two pair of pillow cases, and Josie two dresses, Lillie one and Birdie two and some sunbonnets and underclothes." [11]

Bess Corey, who homesteaded 160 acres alone in South Dakota, wrote her mother frequently of the role of the sewing machine in her life. In 1911 she and neighbor Mae Stone traded work, making dresses for the Stone children, whom she nicknamed the pebbles. "I did the machine work while Mrs. Stone and Florence did the handwork so we got through early." As a schoolteacher she boarded with rural families, living in close quarters in tiny

FIGURE 6.
Sales personnel pose outside a machine dealer's shop, about 1907. Private collection.
Although Singer dominates the advertising here, this dealer also sold Wheeler and Wilson machines, Singer's biggest rival. Women demonstrators had long been an important part of Singer's sales strategy.

FIGURE 7.
Seamstresses in Eskridge, Kansas, pose with their treadle machine in a dressmaking shop in 1896. Private collection.

16

PLATE 7.
Trade card for the New Home sewing machine.
Private collection.

"The White is King of all Sewing Machines"
C-797   1,500,000 NOW IN USE.

PLATE 8.
Trade card for the White sewing machine.
Private collection.

PLATE 9.
Trade card for the Household
sewing machines. Private collection.
Nearly all American machines
have been manufactured east of
the Mississippi, but Western
women long have been served
by dealers in Western cities.
This card informed
Californians where they might
buy a Household brand
machine.

shacks during the school year. "I don't know how I'll like it here," she wrote, "have a room all to myself—it contains a wardrobe, small bed, commode, dresser, chair and sewing machine. It has two windows and no door so everything can come in that wants to and that darn dog Gumbo will sleep in my bed, He is just full of fleas, so I've had a lively time the past 24 hours." [12] Despite her anxieties about her situation, she had one luxury—a sewing machine.

As a single woman on a teacher's meager salary, she could not buy her own machine until 1916. She shared it with her younger brother. "Chall brought me up Sunday . . . and took my sewing machine home with him. He said he'd have his sewing all done up when I came home again, but I couldn't get him to offer to do any of mine." [13]

Chall seems to have been ignorant of the practice of sewing "on shares," in which the woman who borrowed the machine sewed for the machine's owner. Sophie Bost, a Swiss immigrant in Minnesota, described a common kind of trade for work in a letter to her husband's parents in 1869. "I'll be very pleased when I have a machine of my own because that will save me the trouble of having to knit for Mrs. Powers so she can sew for me whatever doesn't have to be done by hand." Sophie's longing for a machine of her own went unfulfilled for three more years, despite more than one such hint to her in-laws. [14]

In a fictionalized memoir, *Sod and Stubble,* John Ise described the coming of the machine to his central Kansas community. "The Bartsches had the only one . . . . [Rosie] paid fifty cents a yard for the work too—a cent a yard for the stitching."

When Rosie finally got her own machine, "It was the only good one in the neighborhood and neighbors from every direction brought their sewing to her . . . . The sewing machine was in a real sense a community institution." [15]

Another Kansan remembered, "Mrs. Erwin had the first sewing machine in the settlement, and in spite of the fact that she was very busy, nearly all the women of the community brought their sunbonnets, which were the most popular head adornment

17

of those days, to her to be machine sewed and quilted. One woman, when she came for her finished
bonnet, was disappointed when it was not starched
and done up ready for her to wear home." [17]

Prices continued to drop through the end of the
century as competition increased. By 1870, there
were sixty-nine American manufacturers. Singer's
major competitors were Wheeler and Wilson, who
had dominated the market in the 1850s and '60s,
and Willcox and Gibbs. Manufacturers multiplied in
the 1870s with familiar names like New Home and
White, which began in 1876. Foreign machines such
as Viking (Husqvarna) from Sweden, which began
producing machines in 1871, competed with the
dominant American companies in Europe and the
rest of the world. During the 1870s, American factories produced three-quarters of a million
machines per year. By 1880, 124 manufacturers
made machines, many of them long-forgotten lines
named Little Wonder and Little Worker, New
Boston and New Buckeye, the Fairy and the Ten
Dollar Novelty.

Ten dollars was cheap; functional machines
never dropped below the $30 to $50 range.
Wisconsin farm woman Helen Olson Halvorsen
recalled that when she married in 1884, she brought
to housekeeping a few comforters she had pieced
and quilted, glass dishes and tin knives, forks and
spoons for six, some gray linen and a sewing
machine. "I had put up ten dollars into that and
mother gave the rest of the money it cost—I think
about $30 or $35." [17]

Helen's machine almost certainly had a treadle,
since electrified machines really were not functional
until the twentieth-century and hand-cranked ones
were old-fashioned in 1884. It may have had a bobbin and an upper spool of thread, which sews the
double-threaded, interlocked stitch patented by
Howe in 1844. His needle with the eye at the point
was the standard for Singers, Wheeler and Wilson
and many other manufacturers.

But Helen's new machine might have been a
chain-stitch model with a tiny hook instead of a
needle. Chain-stitch machines competed healthily
with Howe's interlocked stitch throughout the nine-

FIGURE 8. Private collection.
A Singer salesroom, about 1950.

18

FIGURE 9.

A quilt pattern cut from a Willcox and Gibbs brochure.

Private collection.

The company began manufacturing chain-stitch machines in 1857.

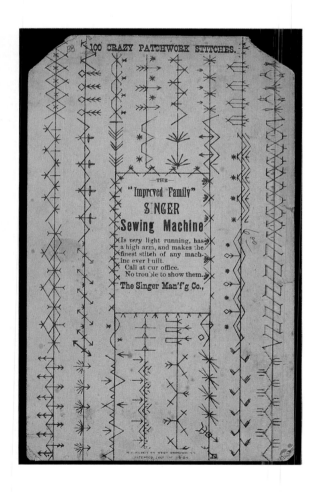

PLATE 10.

Trade Card. Private collection.

The fancy stitches shown on the back of this trade card were popular for crazy quilts in the 1880s and 1890s. The stitches were embroidered by hand, but the machine freed women from plain sewing so they had time for such fancy work.

teenth-century. The giant Willcox and Gibbs Company that specialized in chain-stitch machines strenuously advertised the advantages: the chain stitch used only one thread; there was no bobbin; seamstresses did not have to worry about adjusting the tension or running out of bobbin thread. The disadvantage, pointed out often in competitor's advertising, was that chain stitch machines were slower and the stitch would unravel if broken at any point. Over the long run, Howe's idea won out.

Just as there were two types of machines sold, there were two types of seamstresses, those who whizzed along on the new machinery and those who did not. Among those who did were Sally Baxter Hampton's four sisters-in-law, with whom she lived. She wrote to her sister in 1861, "The girls get on famously with their machine—have no difficulty and make shirts already!!! Always ahead of other people you know." Mary Jones wrote her daughter in 1860, "Yesterday I went to Maxwell to commence my work for Carrie on the machine, but it was quite a failure on my part." In 1859, Ann Lewis Hardeman "passed a rather vexatious day—machine did not do well and my work was not arranged—but at night it seemed well enough though I only tried a small cloth." [18]

The relative ease with which women learned to use the machine may have had something to do with the type of machine they purchased. Willcox and Gibbs's advertising emphasized that even *unskilled* household operators (read "women") could manage their chain-stitch machines. The company's brochures pointed out "the extraordinary demand for our machines, to fill the place of 'first class' double-thread ones, from those who found themselves unable to use the latter with satisfaction." On the other hand, Singer, Wheeler and Wilson and the dozens of other double-thread machine advocates emphasized how easy their machines were to operate despite problems with maintaining equal tension between the top and bottom stitches.

Other factors also influenced ease of use. Hand-cranked machines had to be harder to manage than foot-powered treadles, which freed both hands for guiding. And feeding mechanisms varied considerably. Modern seamstresses take for granted the coordination of needle action with the feed dogs that move the fab-

PLATE 11.
Trade Card. Private collection.
Sewing machine advertising campaigns often implied that those who owned the right machine would have a happy home with well-behaved children and a contented husband.

ric under the presser foot, but imagine machines without feed dogs, presser feet or even a horizontal plate where the fabric rests.

As machines grew easier to use and more available, they began to affect the look of clothing and quilts. Gertrude Clanton Thomas noted changes in fashion in her diary. "Aug. 7 1869. Yesterday I cut out a muslin and today a calico by the princess or gored pattern and have nearly finished both dresses. The long seams are nicely adapted to the machine . . . "[19]

The advent of the machine affected the lives of some women in another profound manner: marketing machines became women's work. Many women found careers in the business world as demonstrators and saleswomen.

A woman identified as Mrs. L.E. Miller is remembered in her 1900 obituary as the first sewing machine agent in the Denver mining country. In 1860 she came west, a single woman in her early twenties, bringing a sewing machine in her covered wagon.

Elizabeth Iliff Warren was another early Denver settler who made a life for herself in the West as a machine saleswoman. Her years working for Singer allowed her to become the best businesswoman, by one contemporary account, in all the West's "stretches of prairies and mountains."

PLATE 12.
Silk quilt and silk dress bodice, 1860s. Collection of Terry Clothier Thompson, Lawrence, Kansas.
Both are constructed with hand seams but machine work dominates in the decorative details of the quilting and the bodice fringe.

PLATE 13.
Detail of *Jackson Star*, by Ellen R.
Eastman Wilson (1843-1927),
Cedar Point, Iowa, 1862.
Hand-pieced and machine-quilted.
Collection of Jeananne Wright,
Longmont, Colorado.
Ellen Eastman was seventeen years
old and teaching at a country
school in Linn County, Iowa,
when she passed her recesses during the Civil War by hand-piecing
this quilt. When she assembled the
blocks, she quilted it on the
machine in a grid pattern typical
of utilitarian machine quilting.

FIGURE 10.
Tintype of an unknown woman, ca. 1870-1875. Private collection.
A dramatic transition in women's fashions occurred after the Civil War.
Both quilts and clothing were affected by the expansion of the machine
into everyday life. In clothing, the wide hoop skirt narrowed to a tight-
fitting dress with a bustle at the back and a draped overskirt. The sewing
machine, which sewed strong seams, allowed for these new vertical lines.
This woman may have made her own dress relying on a machine and
the new proportional pattern systems. Before the advent of the machine
she might have looked to an expert dressmaker who stitched by hand.

Diarists rarely talk about any details of their
quiltmaking, but it is evident from surviving quilts
that several changes occurred after 1870, when the
machine became so widespread. The most visible
change is machine stitching on the surface of the
quilt in appliqué, quilting and binding. Early
machine stitchers were proud of their work. Careful
observation of patterns such as pieced baskets
reveals that quilters approached the use of the
machine in a fashion completely opposite the attitude of today. Nineteenth-century quiltmakers
might use handwork to piece the basket and visible
machine work to appliqué the handle. Today,
machine appliqué is less valued than hand appliqué;
today, most quiltmakers piece the invisible patchwork by machine and appliqué the handle by hand,
so no machine work shows.

Machine quilting is also evident in nineteenth-
century quilts. From the beginning the fact that
quilts could be made by machine was a selling
point. Thomas Saint's original eighteenth-century
patent mentioned quilting. Early machines came
with quilting attachments. In the first decades,
many quilters combined hand and machine quilting, perhaps quilting the edges of the quilt by
machine and the middle by hand. This rather common combination technique probably occurred
because it is difficult to manage the middle of the
heavy quilt under the mechanism, whereas the
edges might be more easily manipulated. Many
children's covers were quilted by machine, probably
because they are easier to manage than full-sized
quilts.

One solution to the bulkiness of quilting was
offered in 1888 by Mrs. J.C., who submitted a
household hint to the *Housekeeper*, a Minnesota
magazine:

> This is the way I do my quilting. I cut the
> top and lining in quarters. Then I lay the
> lining on the table, spread on the cotton,
> baste the top on smooth, and stitch on the
> machine any pattern I please. When the
> four pieces are done, I sew the right
> sides together and fell down the lining
> over the seams and bind the edges. The
> result is much prettier than hand work. [20]

FIGURE 11.
In 1888, Domestic Science students at Kansas State Agricultural College practiced both plain and fancy sewing under the eye of teacher Nellie Sawyer Kedzie, who had to make do with four machines for twelve students. The machines, with their covers neatly at the side, were from the Domestic Sewing Machine Company. Courtesy of the Kansas State Historical Society, Topeka, Kansas.

Machine quilting grew more common in the twentieth century as electrified machines came into use. The nineteenth-century quilts tend to be machine-stitched in straight lines, while designs with curves, such as regular wave patterns and spirals, are twentieth-century work, done on special jigs that attach to the machine. These jigs, which support the quilt as it passes under the needle, appear in advertising in the teens. The data from Kansas Quilt Project documents quilts and quilt-makers from the 1840s through 1988. The records of 4,657 quilted pieces indicate that 527 of them, or 11 percent, were machine-quilted.

The sewing machine also affected the look of borders. Borders of two or three different fabrics tend to date after 1870. Most from that era are hand-stitched, but one can imagine that "the long seams were nicely adapted to the machine," as Gertrude Thomas said of her gored dress. Strip borders became the standard after 1880, when more complex appliquéd and pieced designs faded in popularity.

Three more subtle, but important, changes occurred in quilts. Once machine sewing cut the time devoted to plain sewing, the average woman could do more decorative fancy sewing. It is no

FIGURE 12.
Ora Switzer, Nicodemus, Kansas, 1990. Photo by Barry Worley, Courtesy of the Kansas Quilt Project, Inc. Ora Switzer's *Dresden Plate* is quilted by machine, using a repetitive scroll pattern. Such jig designs are produced by special machine quilting attachments that date from the early twentieth century.

PLATE 20.
Detail of *Cherry Basket Fundraiser*, made by members of the Sunday
School, First Methodist Episcopal Church, Topeka, Kansas, 1883.
Collection of the Kansas State Historical Society, Topeka, Kansas.

PLATE 15.
Trade card. Private collection.
Singer dealer G.A. Bulliss of Grand Island, Nebraska, appealed to
customers with a trade card featuring crazy work.

coincidence that the crazy quilt fad began in the 1880s as machines moved into many American homes. *Scientific American* magazine had predicted the incredible amount of handwork on these embellished, non-functional throws thirty years earlier, when the editors suggested that with the new machines, "Young ladies will have more time to devote to ornamental work (it would be better for them all if they did more of it)." The time devoted to late-Victorian crafts of all kinds, from chip-carved boxes to penny rugs and macramé mantel covers, was time saved from plain sewing. [21]

The abundance and cheapness of fabric in the last quarter of the nineteenth century caused a second significant change in quilts. Machines in factories and homes meant that Americans produced more clothing. More clothing meant a bigger market for calicoes, which dropped in price. More clothing also meant more sewing scraps, saved in the home patch-bag or purchased from clothing manufacturers. An abundance of inexpensive fabric meant more fabric per quilt and smaller pieces. Late-Victorian seamstresses valued tiny scraps rather than tiny stitches, and a multitude of fabrics rather than magnificent quilting. Postage stamp quilts, with their inch-square patches, and charm quilts with no two pieces alike are an indirect result of the machine.

The third, and possibly the most profound, change brought about by the machine was the loss of the hand-sewing skills that were the mark of the cultured woman. Girls born before 1860 spent their childhood and adolescence learning to sew a fine hand. The evidence of their education is in their quilts, especially in the appliquéd extravaganzas made before the Civil War. Once the machine was available, workmanship (workwomanship) steadily declined.

Sarah Jane Full Hill acknowledged a change when she wrote how her machine hummed making tied comforters for Civil War soldiers. When patchwork could be pieced on the machine and tied rather than quilted, quilts became utilitarian items. Quiltmaking skills hit a low in about 1910, when details such as corded binding, elaborate quilting, accurate piecing and appliqué of any kind were almost forgotten. Early twentieth-century quilts that are so casually constructed reflect a generation freed from the role of a human sewing machine, as Tryphena Blanche Fox termed it.

One may mourn the loss of those graceful stitches done by hands trained from childhood, but the words of the women whose lives were changed so deeply make one grateful for the machines that gave later generations independence from the tyranny of the needle and thread.

As the twentieth century passed, quiltmakers developed a new attitude towards the sewing machine and the quilt. In contrast to Mrs. J.C.'s opinion that machine quilting "is much prettier than hand work," twentieth-century seamstresses have tended to hide their machine stitching in the construction. One could acceptably piece and bind a quilt using the machine but the visible stitching *must* be by hand. Visible machine stitching marked a boundary line between fancy quilts and utility quilts. Machine-appliquéd and machine-quilted pieces were considered less attractive, less valuable and finally less authentic.

When Nebraska quiltmaker Ernest Haight decided in 1960 that hand quilting was "slow and tedious," he bought an electric sewing machine and began machine quilting his backlog of tops. He came up against an official description of the conventional wisdom when the managers at the Butler County fair rejected his new pieces as "not art." Eventually they created a new category specifically for machine-pieced quilts, giving him a venue to show his extraordinary work, but continuing the division between hand and machine. This clear-cut division of visible and hidden machine work continues as most contests, fairs and guild shows categorize quilts in such a fashion. The two classes continue, separate and not equal. [22]

Colorado teacher Harriet Hargrave found that quilters considered visible machine work second-rate in the 1980s. As a teacher of machine quilting techniques, she "spent a great deal of time trying to be low profile and not make waves in the hand-quilting world . . . I still remember feeling I had to

PLATE 16.
Whole Cloth Quilt, made by Ada Jones Lewis and Harriet L. Jones, circa 1870. Machine-quilted. Collection of the Oakland Museum of California, Oakland, California.
The makers quilted the name of the sewing machine they used to create this sampler of automated quilting. "American Com.'s Machine" is stitched next to their names. One wonders whether Miss Jones and Mrs. Lewis made the quilt for their own enjoyment or as a commercial venture. Sewing machine companies often hired women to demonstrate the wonders of their product. A quilt such as this would impress many a potential customer.

FIGURE 13.

Practical Machine-Quilting for the Homemaker. Private collection.

Ernest Haight was famous in Nebraska for his intricate machine-piecing.
This 1951 photograph of some blue-ribbon prize winners was on the cover
of his book on machine techniques.

defend and sell the concept."[23]

Many quilters mark 1989 as the beginning of a
new attitude. In that year, Caryl Bryer Fallert's quilt
CoronaII: The Solar Eclipse won the top prize at the
American Quilters' Society's prestigious show in
Paducah, Kentucky. Competing against hand-quilted
work in a show known for its conservative attitude,
Fallert's machine-quilted piece won her a $10,000
purchase award and a place at the center of the
hand-versus-machine controversy. As Hargrave has
written in her influential book, *Heirloom Machine
Quilting,* "Instead of seeing what a magnificent piece it
was regardless of technique, many quilters had trouble
accepting the fact that it was machine quilted . . . I
feel that we spend too much energy debating
whether machine or hand is best." [24]

It has only been in the 1990s, a century and a
half after its invention, that the sewing machine is
finally coming into its own as a tool for quiltmakers. Computerized and electronic machines allow a
wide range of stitch styles. And new accessories like
the walking foot give the operator more control.
But it is primarily a new generation of innovative
artists that has led the way by developing new skills
and techniques, and, most importantly, by teaching
their ideas to wide audiences through writing and
traveling.

Some contemporary innovators use the machine
to imitate the look of hand-sewing. Tricks such as
using invisible thread can mock hand appliqué with
amazing fidelity. Others flaunt the machine stitch,
reveling in the look. They lavish the surface of the
quilt with the tight, continuous stitch and delight in
the tails of thread and the skips left when the needle is removed from the cloth. Such artists as
Therese May and Libby Lehman use the stitch to
add life and shape, color and texture to their textile
compositions.

Contemporary quiltmakers also are exploring
new construction methods using the machine
stitch, exploiting its characteristics—especially its
strength. Unlike hand stitching, the interlocked
machine stitch can be cut without raveling. The
strength of the stitch allows new techniques such as
string piecing, strip piecing, quick piecing, clothes-

line piecing and paper piecing, names quite familiar to machine quiltmakers. These permit an accuracy and complexity that is one of the hallmarks of the late twentieth-century quilt.

Many of these new techniques have roots in traditional sewing. In paper piecing one stitches the fabric to a paper pattern, which is later ripped off. The technique, which is remarkably accurate, is a variation of the foundation piecing that post-Civil War quiltmakers used with Log Cabin and Crazy quilts. In strip piecing the artist stitches strips of fabric together, cuts across them and reconstructs new strips, a technique that is a direct descendent of the Seminole Piecing that Florida tribes have been using for their clothing since 1920.

Quilters have known about fast piecing methods for decades, but it is only recently that they have become part of the working repertoire of nearly all in touch with the commercial network of books, magazines, shops and classes. And it is that very efficient network that makes it all possible.

In 1974 Ernest Haight published a twelve-page pamphlet he sold for $1.50 through the mail. His two-page section called "Some 'Short-cuts' In Piecing Certain Patterns" contained the seeds of the second machine revolution, sketching in a few drawings the mass-production methods we so take for granted. He outlined methods for piecing squares, rectangles and right angles. Among the few that came across Haight's book were Robbie Fanning and Barbara Johannah. Gifted with a mechanical eye, each saw the possibilities and each published her own book on machine techniques in the early 1980s. Their work, in turn, has inspired a pyramid of quilters, designers and teachers who inspire others.

Back in 1974 Haight advised quilters on the importance of a good pair of scissors for the layered cutting he advised. He had never heard of rotary cutters, which have also done their part to change the way quilts look. Like the sewing machine, the rotary cutter is a faster tool, one that allows mass production. Other important technological advances in the past decade include tools as complex as the computer and the photocopy machine and as simple as freezer paper, a coated paper that can be pressed to fabric to stabilize it.

The quilts selected for *Patterns of Progress: Quilts in the Machine Age* show a range of sewing technology. A few contemporary artists work completely by hand; others work completely by machine; many combine techniques. Some of their quilts are traditional in look as well as in technology. Judy Severson and Leslie Pappas echo the nineteenth-century, repeating such conventional patterns as square blocks within a framework of borders. Others, like Caryl Bryer Fallert and Erika Carter, owe more of a design debt to abstract expressionist painting than Pennsylvania German appliqué.

Yet one cannot always link traditional techniques to traditional design. Joe Cunningham's work deconstructs traditional design with magnificent hand quilting. Harriet Hargrave and her student Carolyn Miller reinterpret the best of the nineteenth-century with their computerized machines. At the end of the century, quilters are heading in many directions, guiding their needles with both thimbles and mechanical foot feeds.

ENDNOTES

[1] Letter from Georgia Whitwell in Mary Rathbone Acker, *My Dearest Anna, Letters of the Richmond Family, 1836-1898* (Chicago: Adams Press, 1981), pp. 42-43, quoted in Lynn A. Bonfield, "The Production of Cloth, Clothing and Quilts in Nineteenth Century New England Homes," *Uncoverings 1981* (San Francisco: American Quilt Study Group, 1982), p. 89.

[2] "The Gregson Memoirs," *California Historical Society Quarterly*, Volume 19, Number 2, June 1940, p. 126.

[3] Elizabeth N. Martin (ed.), "The Hulbert Walker Letters: To California via Nicaragua In 1852," *California Historical Society Quarterly*, Volume 36, Number 2, June, 1957, pp. 133-148.

[4] Ann Lewis Hardeman's diary is published in *An Evening When Alone: Four Journals of Single Women in the South,* Michael O'Brien. ed. (Charlottesville, Virginia: University Press of Virginia, 1993) pp. 257-8.

[5] The Jones family letters are published as *The Children of Pride: A True Story of Georgia and the Civil War,* Robert Manson Myers, ed. (New Haven: Yale University Press, 1972), p. 282, p. 507, pp. 501-2.

[6] Rosina Klinger's letters are published in *News From the Land of Freedom: German Immigrants Write Home,* Walter D. Kamphoefner, ed. (Ithaca: Cornell University Press, 1991), p. 558.

[7] Sarah Jane Full Hill's memoirs are published as *Mrs. Hill's Journal: Civil War Reminiscences,* Mark M. Krug, ed. (Chicago: R.R. Donnelley & Sons, 1980), p. 49. Sarah Morgan, diary entry for September 3, 1862, *The Civil War Diary of Sarah Morgan,* Charles East, ed., (Athens: University of Georgia, 1991), p. 234.

[8] Abbie Bright's diary entry for October 14, 1871, "Diary of Abby Bright," Joseph Snell, ed, *Kansas Historical Quarterly,* Fall and Winter, 1971, Volume 37 and 38, p. 417. Elise Dubach Iseley, *Sunbonnet Days* (Caldwell, Idaho: Caxton Printers, 1935), p. 217.

[9] Malinda Jenkins's memoirs are published in *So Much to Be Done: Women Settlers on the Mining and Ranching Frontier,* Ruth B. Moynihan, Susan Armitage, and Christiane Fischer Dichamp, ed. (Lincoln: University of Nebraska Press, 1990), p. 179. Mrs. Conrad Sickles, "Pioneer Years in the Yakima Valley," *Northwest Legacy,* Volume 1, Number 1, September, 1975, pp. 79-102, p. 90.

[10] U. S. Census Reports, Volume 7, Manufacturers, 12th Census, Washington, D. C. 1902, p. 390.

[11] Gertrude Nutter's diary is published in the Cuba, Kansas, Centennial publication, *Lest We Forget,* Glen Lojka, ed. (Cuba, Kansas: n d.), pp. 23-4.

[12] Letter from Bess Corey, September 5, 1911, published as *Bachelor Bess: The Homesteading Letters of Elizabeth Corey, 1909-1919,* Phillip L. Gerber, ed. (Iowa City: University of Iowa Press, 1992), p. 155.

[12] Letter from Bess Corey, December 5, 1916, p. 326.

[14] Sophie Bost's letters are published as *A Frontier Family in Minnesota: Letters of Theodore and Sophie Bost 1851-1920,* Ralph H. Brown, ed. (Minneapolis: University of Minnesota Press. 1981), p. 291.

[15] John Ise, *Sod and Stubble* (Lincoln: University of Nebraska Press, 1967; reprint of the 1936 edition), p. 81-2.

[16] *Dickinson County Historical Sketches,* Volume 3, p 11. Manuscript Collection, Kansas State Historical Society, Topeka Kansas.

[17] Helen Olson Halvorsen's memoirs are published as "Nineteenth-Century Midwife: Some Recollections," in *The Oregon Historical Quarterly,* LXX, Number 1, March. 1969, p. 39-49, p. 43.

[18] Sally Baxter Hampton's letters are published as *A Divided Heart: Letters of Sally Baxter Hampton 1853-1862,* Ann Fripp Hampton, ed. (Spartanburg S.C.: The Reprint Company, 1980), p. 99. Letter from Mary Jones, August 9, 1860, pp. 601-602. Ann Lewis Hardeman's diary entry, February 25, 1859, p. 295.

[19] Gertrude Clanton Thomas's diary is published as *The Secret Eye: The Journal of Ella Gertrude Clanton Thomas,* 1848-1889, Virginia Ingraham Burr, ed. (Chapel Hill: The University of North Carolina Press, 1990), pp. 350-61.

[20] Mrs. J.C., in the *Housekeeper,* Minneapolis. Minnesota. Quoted in the *Colorado Prospector* n.d., p. 6.

[21] *Scientific American,* July 17, 1852, quoted in the *Annual Report of the Smithsonian Institution 1929* (Washington, D.C.: U.S. Government Printing Office, 1930), pp. 582-3.

[22] Haight, *Practical Machine-Quilting for the Homemaker* (David City, Nebraska: 1974).

[23] Harriet Hargrave, *Heirloom Machine Quilting* (Martinez, California: C & T, 1996), p. 5.

[24] Hargrave. *Heirloom Machine Quilting,* p. 5.

PLATE 17. STAR MEDALLION QUILT,
made by an ancestor of Barbara Jackson, 1825-1850.
88 x 93 inches.
Hand-pieced, hand-stuffed and hand-quilted.
Collection of Barbara and Kern Jackson, Arkansas.

This star quilt, made before the advent of the sewing machine, is a tour-de-force of hand workmanship. Virginia Gunn, costume historian and quilt historian, has pointed out the parallels between clothing and quilt construction in the years before the machine. The delicate stitches used to piece the stars were the basic method of assembling clothing by hand. The seam allowance that quilters still use—one-quarter of an inch—was the standard when the selvage edges of cloth were much narrower. Little girls were taught to make quilts as practice for their life work of stitching clothing. A masterpiece such as this showed off a woman's needlework skills indicating she had learned her childhood lessons well.

29

PLATE 18. APPLIQUÉ SAMPLER,
made by a member of the Fitzsimmons family, possibly in Jacksonville, Illinois, 1840-1865.
80 x 85 inches.
Hand-appliquéd and hand-quilted.
Collection of Barbara and Kern Jackson, Arkansas.

Another quilt belonging to the Jackson family, made before the sewing machine began to dominate home sewing, is a sampler both of appliqué designs and hand sewing techniques. The appliqué is tacked with a fine buttonhole stitch over raw edges. The piping tucked into the binding is common in clothing made during the Civil War era, when women inserted covered cording into the seams of bodices and sleeves. Quilts often reflect clothing fashion of the time.

The design looks to be a one-of-a-kind assemblage of blocks and border, but several nearly identical quilts have been discovered. The similarity of a group of quilts with a central wreath, corner blocks of floral sprays, and a border of urns and trailing vines, might suggest that the makers were relatives, neighbors, or students at the same school. The quilts, however, were made from West Virginia to Illinois, mostly along the fortieth parallel, the line of western migration across the United States. One can imagine migrating women showing their quilts to new friends as they moved west, leaving behind a hand-drawn pattern. This quilt came west with descendants of the maker, who now live in Arkansas.

PLATE 19. FLORAL BASKET,
made by Mary Parks Lawrence (1854-1950), Logan County, Kentucky, 1870.
72 x 84 inches.
Hand-and machine-appliquéd; hand- and machine-quilted.
Collection of the Wichita-Sedgwick County Historical Museum,
Wichita, Kansas.
Gift of Marjorie Caskey.

Mary Parks carried this quilt west when she came to Sumner County, Kansas, with her parents to homestead in 1878. She made it when she was sixteen, using the sewing machine her father provided in exchange for her promise to stitch coats for her brothers. The family still remembers what a great day it was in 1870 when the machine arrived.

The quilt tells a tale of the mid-century transition from the hand to the machine age. Mary traded her handwoven fabrics for the factory-woven cottons in the quilt. She combined hand and machine sewing, using the new machine where it was most functional, and quite visible. Both techniques were equally valuable to her.

Mary's sense of symmetry is worth noting. She cut three of her basket blocks in half, presumably because she wanted a quilt of a certain size and never thought about pictorial composition. A photograph of her daughter Eunice, taken in the early twentieth century, shows how Mary used the quilt to make her bed. The half blocks are tucked under the foot of the mattress.

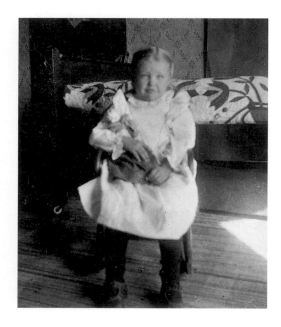

PLATE 20. CHERRY BASKET FUNDRAISER,
made by members of the Sunday School, First Methodist Episcopal Church,
Topeka, Kansas, 1883.
74 x 72 1/2 inches.
Hand-pieced, machine-appliquéd, hand-quilted, hand-inked.
Collection of the Kansas State Historical Society, Topeka, Kansas.

Women have long made quilts to raise money for charitable causes such as
Indian missions or church building projects. Red and white were favorite colors for fundraisers. This quilt, made by the women of the city of Topeka, is a
rather elegant example of the type. The beautiful hand-quilted feathers are
embellished with dozens of names. Each person made a donation in order to
have his or her name included. Names at the center of a circle usually cost
more than the names in the ring. When the quilt was finished and the money
counted, the women gave the quilt to W.D. Gossett, the superintendent of the
Sunday School. It is a wonderful record of life in Topeka in the early 1880s.

The pieced basket pattern was popular after the 1850s. Many women
hand-pieced the triangles in the basket and machine appliquéd the handles,
indicating an acceptance of visible machine stitching that confuses some who
consider themselves traditionalists. Most contemporary quilters would hide
their machine work in the seams of the triangles and hand-appliqué the handles.

Art Center College of Design
Library
1700 Lida Street
Pasadena, Calif. 91103

PLATE 21. CHILD'S HANDS,

made by Amanda Elizabeth Garman, Kill Creek Community,
Douglas County, Kansas, about 1878.
37 x 32 1/2 inches.
Machine-pieced, hand-appliquéd and machine-quilted.
Collection of the Kansas State Historical Sociery, Topeka, Kansas.

The family story is that Amanda Garman made this small quilt, with its delicate sashing, for daughter Bertha, born in 1878. She traced around the baby's
tiny hand for the pattern. Bertha's baby quilt is always a favorite when on display. Many quilt lovers, however, express disappointment when they examine
the quilt closely and realize it is machine-quilted; they feel that Amanda
Garman spoiled an otherwise great quilt with her sewing machine. Such an
attitude regarding antique quilts is reflected in monetary value as well as aes-
thetics: machine-quilted antiques are generally worth less than hand-quilted
ones. Sometimes it is difficult to think of these machine-made quilts in the
context of their time and through the eyes of the maker, who must have been
quite pleased with her new machine.

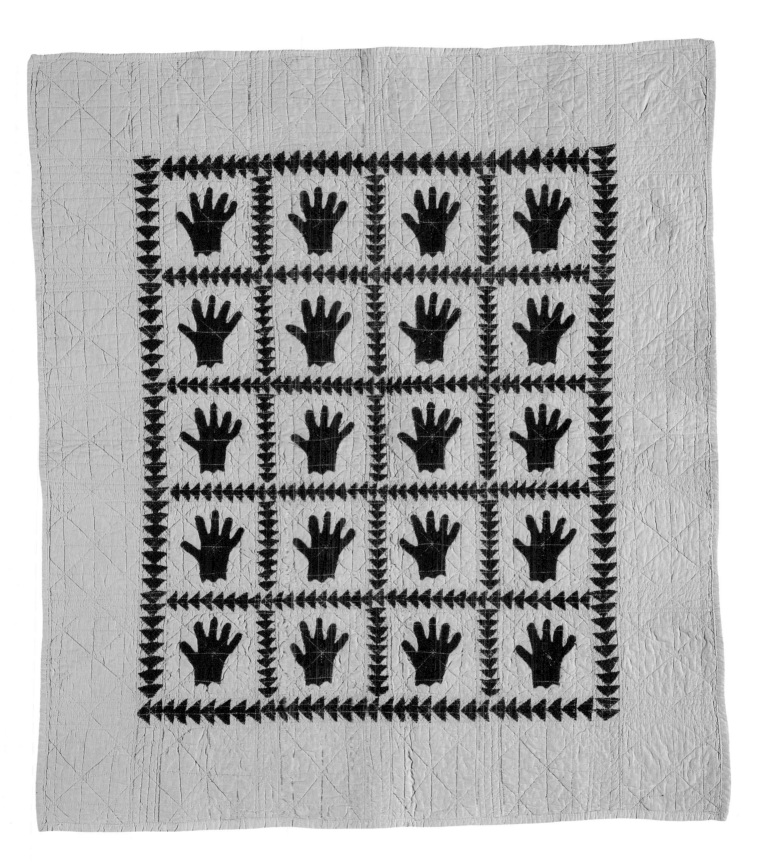

PLATE 22. WHIG ROSE,
maker unknown, 1870-1900.
70 x 80 inches.
Hand-appliquéd and hand-quilted.
Collection of the Autry Museum of Western Heritage, Los Angeles, California.
Acquisition made possible by the Glendale Quilt Guild.

The *Whig Rose* pattern was named after the political party powerful in the years when the design developed in the 1840s. Quilt pattern historians speculate that this version of the rose, with the feathery combs circling the central flower, was known as the *Democrat Rose*. Long before the donkey symbolized the Democrats, a rooster was printed on ballots for the illiterate voter. The floral combs recall the rooster. The *Whig Rose* was similar, but it lacked the combs.

The only clues to the date of this quilt are in the way it looks and the way it was made. Because it is bound by sewing machine, it was likely finished after the mid–1850s when the machine moved into homes. While the design dates to the 1840s, this version was probably made after the Civil War, when the sewing machine and synthetic dyes changed the textile industry so dramatically. One subtle, yet important, clue is the double border of two strips. These rather simple borders became quite popular after the 1870s, when both quilt and dress design reflected the sewing machine's ability to stitch long, strong seams.

The tan fabric may have once been green. Green was a particularly difficult color to obtain in cottons at the time, whether dyers used natural dyes or the new synthetic colors. Laundry and light were likely to change dark forest greens to this drab khaki. This green has the look of a faded synthetic dye, developed after 1870.

The quilt probably is not a twentieth-century piece. By 1900 American seamstresses had tired of appliqué design and no longer had the sewing skills to produce such quilts. A critical view of the appliqué, quilting and design in this piece reveals a certain lack of skill and grace that reflects the post-machine decline in needlework. The combination of fabric, technique and design indicate a date of 1870 to 1900.

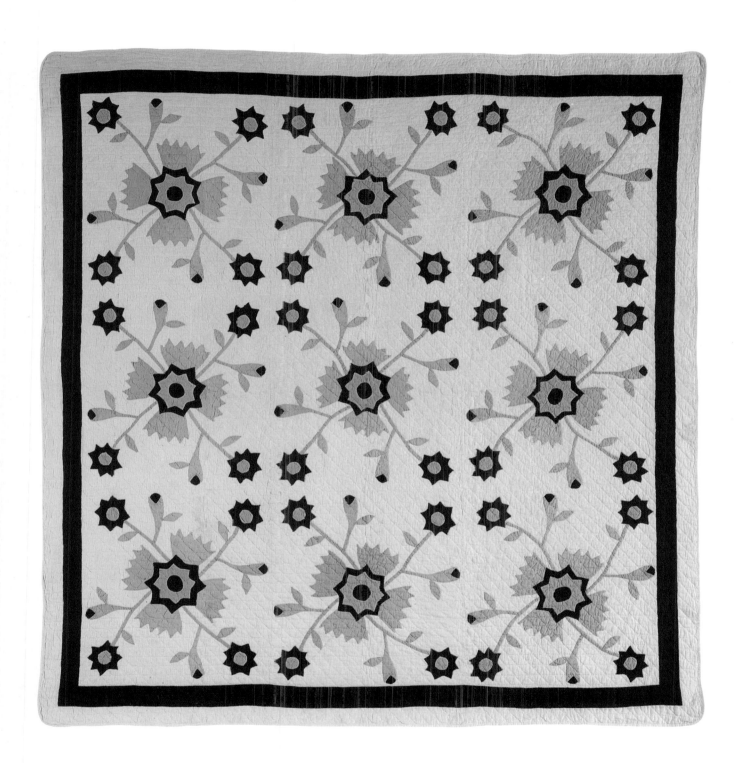

PLATE 23. SWALLOW'S NEST OR SINGING CORNERS,
maker unknown, 1890-1925.
66 x 76 1/2 inches.
Hand- and machine-pieced and machine-quilted.
Collection of Jennifer Carr Kinney.

Once the sewing machine changed women's lives, needlework skills were almost forgotten. At the turn of the last century, when this piece was made, quilts were often poorly constructed in rather simple designs. While quilts were quite common, appliqué, fine quilting and skillful piecing were rare. This quilt, then, is rather exceptional in its precision and grace.

At the time the quilt was made, the pattern was sold under the names *Swallow's Nest* or *Singing Corners*. It is a variation of *Turkey Tracks* or *Wandering Foot*. Most quilters know about the story of the Wandering Foot design during the years of westward expansion, when so many young men left their mothers behind in search of fortune. No quiltmaker would make a bedcover of this design for her son, since sleeping under it was guaranteed to give him a case of wanderlust.

PLATE 24. SISTER'S CHOICE,
maker unknown, 1890-1925.
76 x 63 inches.
Machine- and hand-pieced, machine-quilted.
Collection of Jennifer Carr Kinney.

Like fashions in clothing and interiors, quilt fashions change. This quilt, with its blues, grays and maroon prints, is a perfect example of the kind so fashionable a century ago. The pattern is relatively complex, but it is made of simple pieces that required little sewing skill. *Sister's Choice* is one name published in the pattern catalogues of the time. The blocks are set apart and bordered with strips of sashing, a popular look once the sewing machine encouraged long seams. The machine quilting is utilitarian rather than fancy, but such quilts rarely left space for fancy quilting.

One might think that these quilts, which look so plain to modern eyes, were made just for warmth, but it is important to realize that the quiltmaker made many aesthetic choices. She picked the brand new colors in printed cottons, she selected (and possibly paid a dime for) a popular and innovative pattern, and she set and finished the quilt with a symbol of her status, her sewing machine.

43

PLATE 25. BULLET/RIN TIN TIN,
maker unknown, 1950-1965.
79 x 79 inches.
Hand-embroidered, hand-quilted.
Collection of the Autry Museum of Western Heritage, Los Angeles, California.

Bullet was cowboy star Roy Rogers' dog, a clever German Shepherd who saved many a day on the popular television show. Little is known about this quilt that depicts the dog and his master. It also portrays Rin Tin Tin and his young master from that television series. The blocks were probably traced from coloring books or comics of the era, although it is possible that there was a commercial pattern specifically sold for embroidery.

This type of pictorial quilt developed about 1880, as magazines developed the technology for printing iron-on transfers. The patterns featured only the design outline, suggesting that the needleworker fill it in with colored stitches. But the audience liked the look of the outline (and it was far less work than filled embroidery), so outline embroidered designs have been a quiltmaking standard for more than a century. The designs were a popular way to teach girls to embroider as late as the 1950s. Anyone who labored over her stitches as a child will appreciate the amount of handwork in the sixty-four blocks.

PLATE 26. FALLING BLOCKS,
made by Ernest B. Haight, David City, Butler County, Nebraska, ca. 1970.
76 x 99 inches.
Machine-pieced and machine-quilted.
Collection of the American Museum of Quilts and Textiles.

Ernest Haight, trained as an agricultural engineer in the 1920s, spent his life as a farmer. He began making quilts in his thirties, during the Depression, when quilt-making was quite popular. After he complained to his wife about the inaccuracies of her grandmother's piecing, Isabelle Hooper Haight challenged him to do better. He pieced his first quilt top on the treadle machine that his grandparents had brought to Nebraska in 1880.

Ernest and his father Elmer collaborated for years, with the elder Haight hand-quilting his son's machine-pieced tops. Ernest's mother and his wife also quilted, but none of the family could keep up with his production. In 1960 he decided that hand quilting was too "slow and tedious," and bought a new electric machine to teach himself to machine quilt. Butler County Fair officials rejected the machine-quilted pieces because they were "not art," but soon created a new category especially for his work. His machine techniques impressed state fair officials enough that they encouraged him to write a book explaining his methods. He published *Machine Quilting for the Homemaker* in 1974 and sold it for $1.

With his engineer's training, Haight may have been the first to develop machine-based methods of construction that went beyond imitating the hand stitch. At any rate, he seems to have been the first to write about it. He outlined methods for strip-piecing squares and rectangles and speed-piecing right triangles, ideas that are the basis of the mass-production methods quilters take for granted today.

Falling Blocks is one of his hundreds of quilts. He truly loved to sew, to teach and to talk about his work. In an interview in 1982, he described how much he enjoyed using his sewing machine:

You talk about hand sewing being relaxing. I used to work with machinery all day. I'd come in at 9:00 dead tired from milking cows and sit down at the sewing machine and sew for an hour.

When I was done I'd have to force myself to go to bed.

This quilt is typical of Haight's machine work. The fabric is what he found at the local dry goods store. He often inserted black outlines around his blocks, shaving a 1/16 inch off each. He liked the dark frame and was proud of his accuracy. The blocks were pieced as strips and then cut to the correct size, using one of his shortcuts, now known as strip-piecing. The unusual set reflects his drafting and piecing skills as well as his engineer's eye.

PLATE 27. HAPPY TIME OF LEAVES AND
BERRY BLOSSOMS,
made by Ella First Kill Brown, Gros Ventre, 1970-1993.
91 x 82 1/2 inches.
Machine-pieced and hand-quilted.
Collection of the Autry Museum of Western Heritage, Los Angeles, California.

The block design is an old one, known in the mainstream quilt world by names such as *Goose Tracks* or *Dove in the Window*. Ella First Kill Brown's name reflects her Native American interpretation of pattern and color. Ella's love of colors is reflected in this quilt which evokes the joy in spring's fruit blossoms. Native Americans often turn to the environment for design ideas and color schemes for their quilts. The techniques Ella chose are typical of American pieced quilts in the past few decades. She has pieced the invisible patchwork seams by machine and finished the quilt with visible hand quilting.

PLATE 28. LATE FALL TIME,
made by Josephine Red Elk, Lakota Sioux, 1970-1993.
106 x 87 inches.
Machine-pieced and hand-quilted.
Collection of the Autry Museum of Western Heritage, Los Angeles, Califonia.

Many American quilt designs are based on an eight-pointed star. These large central stars, known to mainstream quilters as the *Star of Bethlehem* or the *Lone Star*, have been popular since the 1830s. Known by the Sioux as the *Morning Star*, this design has been depicted on quilts, clothing, moccasins and hide paintings. Star quilts are now an important part of their gift-giving culture. Josephine Red Elk used a sewing machine to piece her star, which was inspired by autumn's colors.

PLATE 29. GOLDEN GLOW,
made by Blanche Young, Los Angeles, California, 1995.
78 x 93 inches.
Machine-pieced and machine-quilted.
Collection of the maker.

Blanche Young and her daughters have had enormous impact upon quiltmaking through their books and teaching. Inspired by the strips of tiny patchwork that Seminole and Miccosukee tribes use to decorate their clothing, the Youngs have developed methods of fast piecing for traditional patterns. *Golden Glow* is based on a design called *Trip Around the World*, popular in southeastern Pennsylvania, where Amish and Pennsylvania German women mark and cut each square. In their "New Approach," Blanche and her daughters advocate thinking in terms of rows, cutting across machine stitching to reassemble the finished pattern.

PLATE 30. SCRAP BROKEN STAR COLOR WHEEL,
made by Blanche Young, Los Angeles, California, 1997.
81 x 80 inches.
Machine-pieced and machine-quilted.
Collection of the maker.

Blanche Young, a true child of the machine age, says she doesn't do anything by hand, "not even dishes." This color study is one of her many star quilts, stitched with her methods of machine piecing strips of fabric and cutting across the strips at a forty-five degree angle. Such star quilts used to be rather unusual as they were considered the mark of an accomplished hand piecer. Following the Youngs' methods, novices have been inspired to get out their machines and successfully tackle such a challenge in a weekend or an afternoon.

PLATE 31. THE PAPER PIECED SUN,
made by Marie Fritz, San Diego, California, 1997.
88 x 88 inches.
Machine-pieced, hand-quilted.
Collection of the maker.

Inspired by an antique quilt, Marie Fritz decided to piece a copy using traditional hand methods and a contemporary color scheme. But as she studied the quilt she realized the spikes could be pieced by machine using a paper pattern for the foundation. She taught herself the basics of what is called "paper piecing" and finished the top in a month. Quilting it by hand took several years.

Paper piecing allows quilters an impressive accuracy with curves and fine points. The accuracy extends to miniatures so many quilters are making complex blocks only three inches square. When quilt historians look back at the 1990s they will note an explosion of complex patterns made with these long triangles, a result of the machine age.

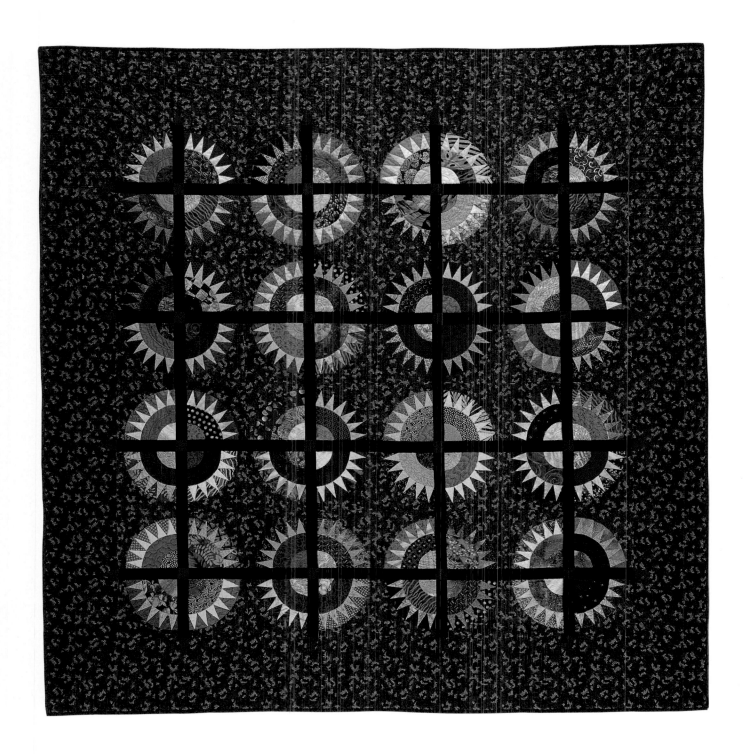

PLATE 32. HANDS IN FRIENDSHIP,
made by Carol Gilham Jones, Lawrence, Kansas, 1995.
75 x 84 inches.
Machine-pieced, machine-appliquéd and machine-quilted.
Collection of the maker.

Carol Jones' friendship quilt was made at a week-long quilting retreat at Point Bonita in Marin County, California. Each woman there traced around her hand and signed it. Erma Kirkpatrick, a regular at the retreat, was unable to attend. Carol mailed her fabric, warning that time was of the essence. If Carol finished the top before Erma replied, her hand would wind up on the back. In an unsuccessful attempt to get her hand on the front, Erma wrote this verse on it:

I understand that, without any guilt,

You're putting my hand on the back of your quilt.

You must select the position, my dear,

A pat on the shoulder or a smack in the rear.

Carol might have hand-appliquéd the sixty-five hands and one dog's paw, but it is unlikely she would have ever conceived of so ambitious a project. Besides increasing the complexity of the design, new techniques of machine appliqué also allow quiltmakers to think in bigger numbers.

PLATE 33. ANTHURIUM,
made by Carol Gilham Jones, Lawrence, Kansas, 1996.
41 x 41 inches.
Machine-pieced, machine-appliquéd and hand-quilted.
Collection of the maker.

When Americans began appliquéing quilts more than 200 years ago, they often cut the flowers from valuable European chintzes, stitching the printed designs into new compositions. The technique, called *Broderie Perse* (Persian Embroidery), fell from favor in the nineteenth century. Carol Jones is staging a one-woman revival, cutting up large scale fabrics in a new version of *Broderie Perse*. In this quilt she has cut up African fabrics, using machine appliqué techniques to easily rearrange the images in any way she likes.

PLATE 34. EDIE'S ANTIQUE STARS,
made by Mabry Benson, Kensington, California, 1997.
68 x 72 inches.
Machine-pieced and machine-quilted.
Collection of the maker.

When friend Edie Brady found an exquisite nineteenth-century quilt top, Mabry Benson decided to copy it. The antique top was a treasure, too old to quilt without damage and too historically valuable to alter. Mabry's machine-made copy combines the best of both centuries, an old-fashioned look with speed-production that takes the preciousness out of the piece. This is a quilt Mabry sleeps under; when it wears out she can easily make another if she chooses. She has also made one for Edie, who now has both the delicate antique and the functional copy.

PLATE 35. OAK LEAVES,
made by Mabry Benson, Kensington, California, 1997.
78 x 82 inches.
Machine-pieced, machine-appliquéd and machine-quilted.
Collection of the maker.

Mabry Benson has created a patchwork carpet of fallen leaves in *Oak Leaves*. Using machine appliqué to anchor the oak leaves, she has added a line and texture unique to the machine stitch. Without a machine she might have appliquéd leaves, but probably a simpler, more stylized version, and certainly far fewer. Machine appliqué is affecting the expressiveness of contemporary artists, reducing old limits of time and detail.

PLATE 36. OHIO ROSE WITH VINE BORDER,
made by Judy Severson, Belvedere, California, and Bettina Havig,
Columbia, Missouri, 1986-1990.
85 x 85 inches.
Hand-pieced, appliquéd and stuffed by Judy and hand-quilted by Bettina.
Collection of Judy Severson.

Both Judy and Bettina persist in making their quilts by hand in the midst of the machine age. Judy says she finds hand work relaxing. "Since I work, the only time I have to make quilts is in the evenings. I like to spend time with my family as I sit and sew. I quilt for myself so there's no reason to hurry."

Bettina speaks of the tactile experience in handwork. "I quilt by hand because I like to do it. I like to feel how it goes together. All I'd get from a machine is vibration and electro-magnetic waves. I love to hand-piece too. Hand-piecing is great conditioning for hand-quilting. If more people pieced by hand they'd find their hand-quilting would be better."

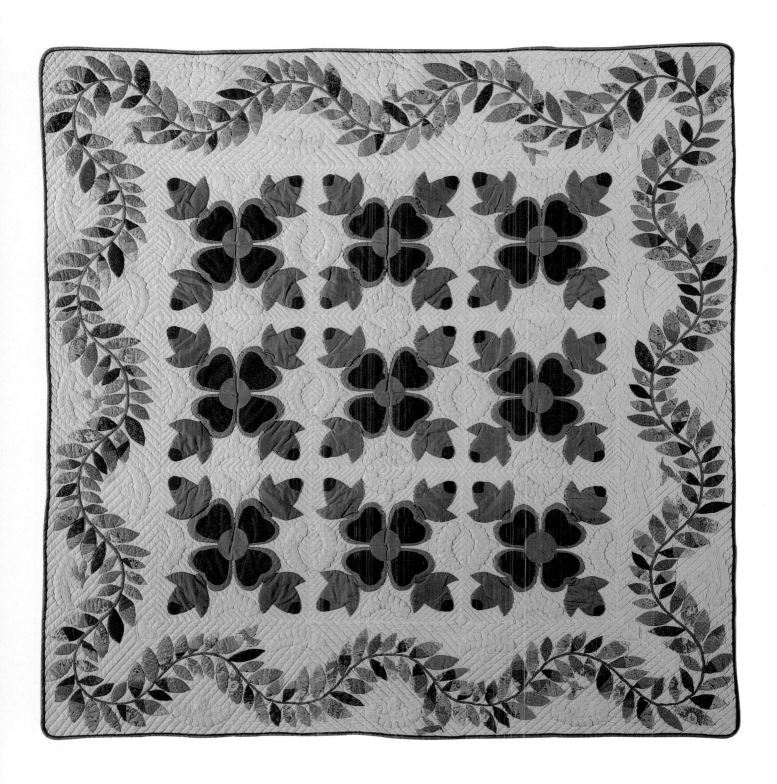

PLATE 37. THIS IS A QUILT, NOT ART,
made by Joe Cunningham, San Francisco, California, 1996.
81 x 61 inches.
Machine-pieced and hand-quilted.
Collection of the maker.

Joe Cunningham's new series deconstructs traditional patchwork, moving
design elements around on the face of the quilt to make a decidedly non-traditional piece. He still lavishes the surface with the hand quilting for which
he is known, proving that traditional methods do not necessarily produce an
old-fashioned look.

PLATE 38. THE PERFECT EXISTENTIAL OBJECT,
made by Joe Cunningham, San Francisco, California, 1997.
69 1/2 x 69 1/2 inches.
Machine-pieced and hand-quilted.
Collection of the maker.

Joe Cunningham is well known for his quilting and his free-hand marking of quilt designs without templates. In a departure from his past work, he no longer marks his quilts as preparation for quilting. Years of experience have allowed him to stitch free-hand in patterns such as feathers and cables. He questions why quilters first draw on the quilt with a pencil or other marking tool when they could directly draw with the needle and thread. How many mid-nineteenth century needlewomen actually marked their quilts? Might these quilters, who learned to sew before they learned to write, have been skillful enough to run their needles along unmarked but very familiar paths?

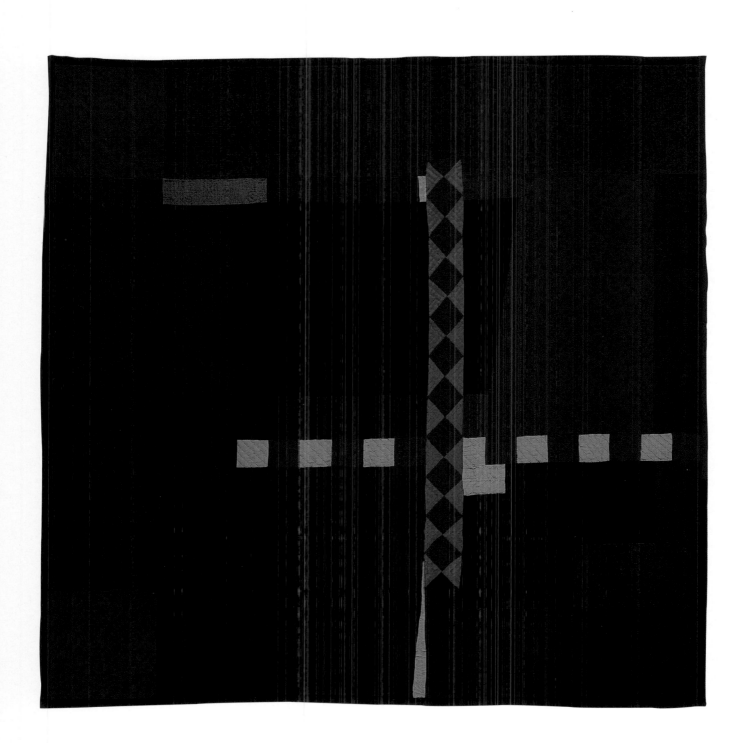

PLATE 39. THE PEOPLE/THE PLACE,
made by Sandi Fox, Los Angeles, California, 1982.
84 x 84 inches.
Hand-pieced, hand-appliquéd, hand-embroidered and hand-quilted.
Collection of the Music Center of Los Angeles County.

Sandi Fox is one of the leading advocates of hand sewing today. This quilt commissioned by the Los Angeles Music Center reflects her devotion to traditional design and technique. The signatures are those of contributors to the Music Center. Sandi obtained the autographs of people from Charlton Heston to Yo Yo Ma, traced them onto fabric and embroidered them with a single strand of sewing thread.

Her classes, in which she emphasizes the hand stitch from block to set to binding, are popular alternatives to the contemporary idea of "making a quilt in an afternoon." For more than twenty years she has taught the series in Utah, traveling from her home in Los Angeles every other month to meet with a group of about sixty women. "The word 'machine,'" laughs student Peggy Childress, who has attended for decades, "is a four-letter word."

Sandi explains her devotion to the hand stitch by saying that it is "a physical experience. I love the unfettered feeling of cloth, the way it feels and smells, the way you can almost hear it move. We celebrate the needle, the number 12 short."

PLATE 40. SUNBURST,
made by Peggy Childress, Provo, Utah, 1994.
63 1/2 x 63 3/4 inches.
Hand-pieced, hand-stuffed and hand-quilted.
Collection of the maker.

Sunburst is a traditional pattern done in a very traditional fashion. Peggy Childress put every stitch in by hand. Why handsew in the 1990s? "I just love handwork. I can be happy anywhere as long as I take my handsewing with me. I can carry everything I need in my pocket." The portability of hand stitching is part of its appeal. "I grew up in an age where you were taught that you don't sit without something to do. We could never just sit. I sew while I watch t.v." Her husband helps out by warning her to look up at the exciting moments. "I can watch football because there are replays, but basketball is harder to keep up." In the age of the instant replay, she chooses to spend her time at handwork, a process many might view as tedious, but one she thinks life would be tedious without.

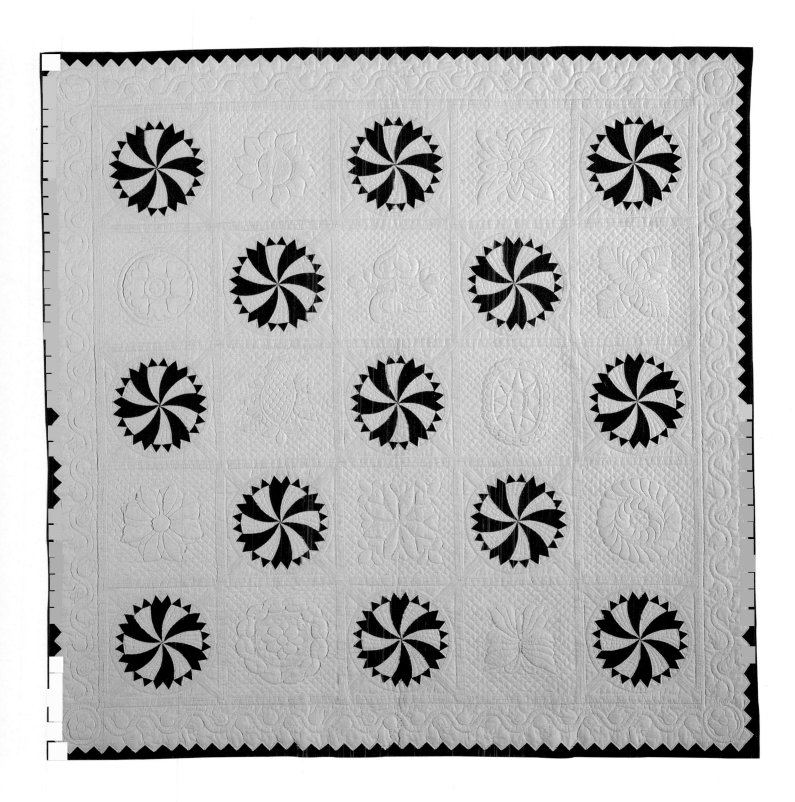

PLATE 41. LOG CABIN: COURTHOUSE STEPS,
made by Leslie Pappas, Salt Lake City Utah, 1995.
70 x 86 inches.
Hand-pieced and hand-quilted.
Collection of the maker.

Leslie looks to antique quilts for inspiration. At first glance the pattern and coloring could be mistaken for a late nineteenth-century piece. Her *Log Cabin* grew from a crib-sized project to a bedcover with almost 6,000 pieces, each one-half inch wide. "If I'd known how big it was going to get I'd probably have used wider strips. But I love the scale of it. It took forever. Three years."

Like other hand stitchers, Leslie mentions the sociability that hand work allows. She also refers to the soothing qualities and tactile sensations she enjoys. "I feel the fabric. I don't just whip it down. I take the time to admire it. I'm in no hurry."

PLATE 42. QUILT HOUSES,
made by Sylvia Taylor, Provo, Utah, 1995.
49 3/4 x 73 1/4 inches.
Hand-pieced and hand-quilted.
Collection of the maker.

Another of Sandi Fox's students, Sylvia Taylor sews quilts exclusively by hand. Like the technique, the coloring in her quilt echoes the past. The blues and plaids revive a look popular at the turn of the twentieth century. The central pattern with its skewed squares also can be found in quilts of that time. It is the same one from which Ernest Haight drew his *Falling Blocks* variation [see Plate 26]. Published names include the Box Quilt or Eccentric Star. Sylvia has brought her handmade quilt up to date by adding a border with the same offbeat repeat.

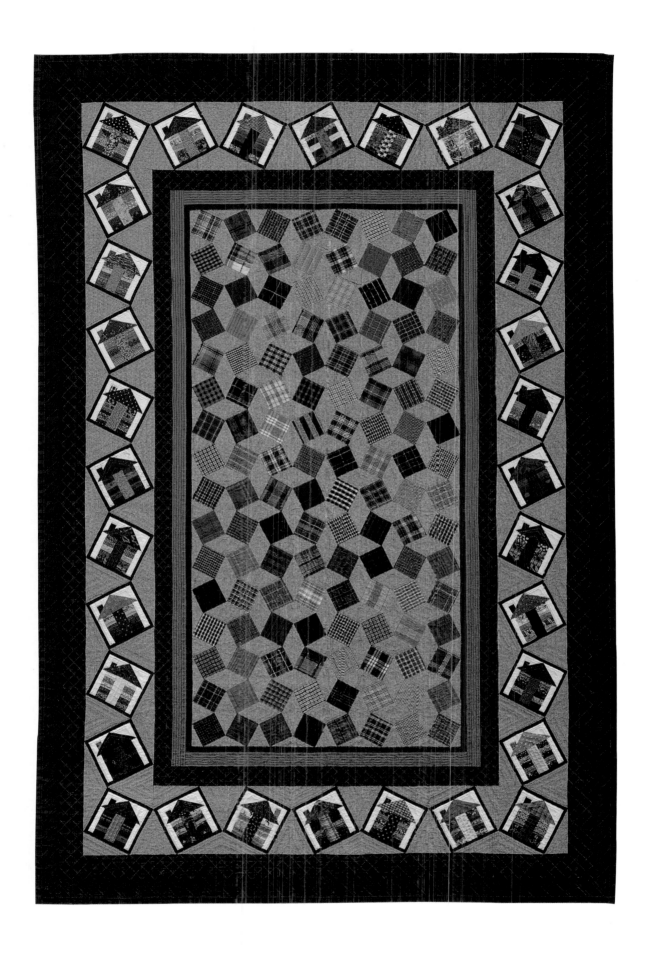

PLATE 43. CLAM CROSSING,
made by Emily Lowe, Salt Lake City, Utah, 1994.
67 3/8 x 67 3/4 inches.
Hand-pieced and hand-quilted.
Collection of the maker.

Emily Lowe is another of the Utah women who enroll in Sandi Fox's continuing classes in traditional hand work. Her handstitched quilt is an example of late twentieth-century design, incorporating the types of color contrasts, pattern and repeat popular with quiltmakers today. Earlier quiltmakers might recognize the individual pattern elements, the stars and fans and border of triangles, but they rarely assembled the units in these clever new ways, fragmenting the block and setting pattern side-by-side to obtain more complex secondary designs. Emily might also surprise them with her reversal of the traditional ratio of block to border size. The elements of the clamshell borders outscale the central design. Borders used to be secondary to the block.

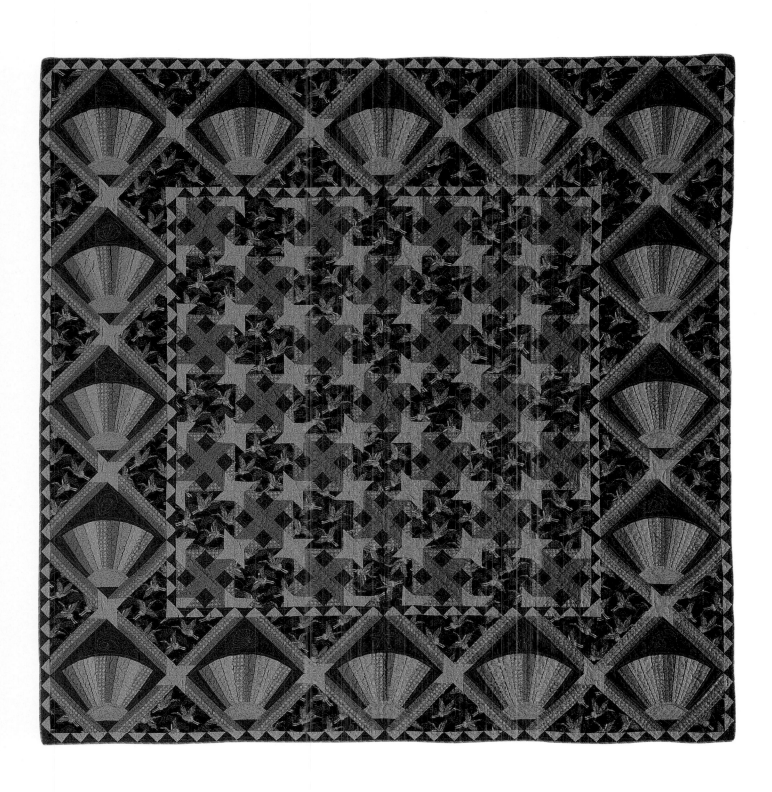

PLATE 44. STARRY PATH,
made by Laura Tomita Lyons, Salt Lake City, Utah, 1995.
41 1/2 x 65 inches.
Hand-pieced and hand-quilted.
Collection of Dr. and Mrs. Ed Bronsky.

Laura Tomita Lyons has combined one of the simplest and oldest of patchwork designs, the *Four Patch*, with a block sold as *Starry Path* in newspapers during the 1930s. The modern looking star was the product of a particularly innovative designer now known only by the pen names of Laura Wheeler and Alice Brooks. Laura Lyons has added a contemporary look to the old blocks with high contrast coloring and an asymmetry uncommon in traditional quilts.

PLATE 45. THE HUNT OF MANY TRIBES,
made by Cordy Sander, Newcastle, California, 1996.
51 x 53 inches.
Machine-pieced and machine-quilted.
Collection of the maker.

Cordy Sander combines Native American imagery with the eight–pointed star that is found in European patchwork dating back centuries. Quilts, like much else in American culture, combine design and form from many cultures.

PLATE 46. BLACK HATS AND WHITE HATS,
made by Cordy Sander, Newcastle, California, 1992.
45 x 45 inches.
Machine-pieced, hand-appliquéd and machine-quilted.
Collection of the maker.

Americans define themselves through a number of images. Two themes that ring throughout our culture are the mythological American West and the mythological American Quilt. Cordy Sander has combined these durable images by layering the symbols of the good cowboy and bad atop a traditional patchwork design. As with all myths, it is difficult to determine reality. What is traditional in patchwork? Things are never so black and white as the cowboy hats would suggest. Cordy combines hand and machine sewing. Is the quilt less authentic or less valuable than the almost mythological handmade object?

PLATE 47. NUCLEAR WHALES IN EDINBURGH,
made by Ann Merrell, Cupertino, California, 1995.
58 x 44 inches.
Machine-pieced and machine-quilted.
Collection of the maker.

A musician for a saxophone group called the Nuclear Whales, Ann Merrell leaves her sewing machine behind when she is on the road. Yet a good percentage of the time devoted to her art is spent finding the right fabrics for the look she wants, so time on tour can be devoted to shopping. The unconventional fabrics for this unconventional quilt were found in Scotland.

She quotes teacher Harriet Hargrave in talking about the status of machine quilting. "'There are enough quilts in all our heads that need to come out, that as long as the workmanship is of high quality, it should not matter what technique was used.' Some of those quilts to which Hargrave refers are in my head, and as I become more proficient in machine quilting, the quilts that would be appropriately machine-quilted will be."

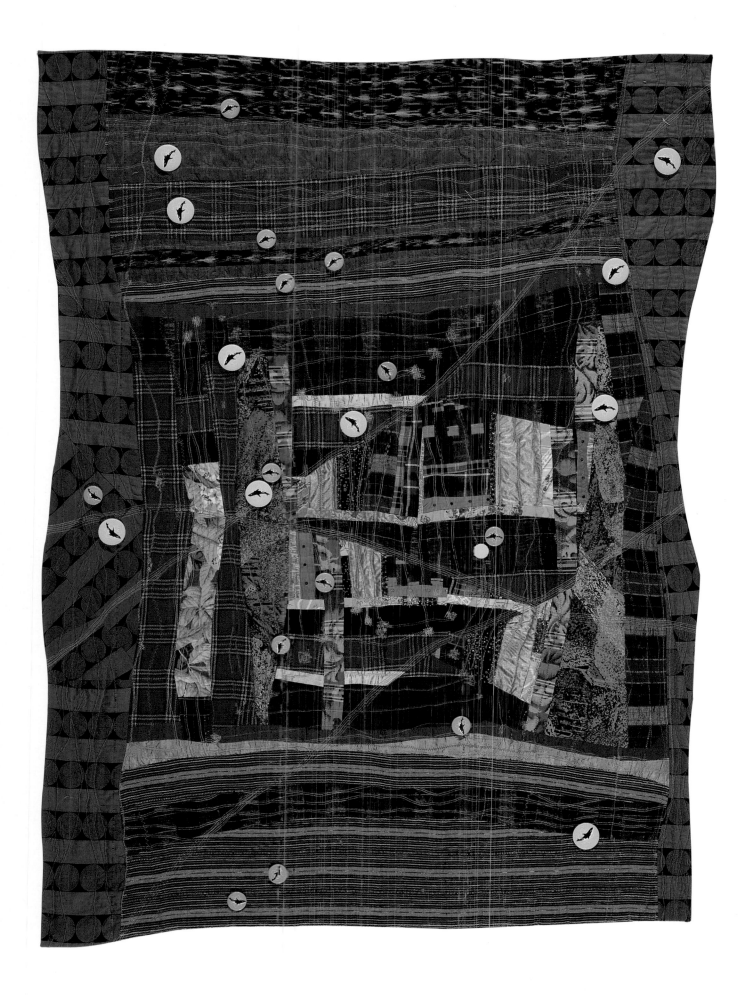

PLATE 48. CO(W)LLABORATION,

made by Ann Merrell and Doreen Speckmann, Cupertino, California and Madison,
Wisconsin, 1997.
38 x 39 inches.
Machine-pieced and machine-quilted.
Collection of Ann Merrell.

Year after year, Ann Merrell and Doreen Speckmann park their sewing
machines near each other at an annual quiltmaking retreat in Marin County,
California. Although their tools are the same, their styles are quite different.
Ann proposed that Doreen piece a small quilt top in her typical style, a contemporary take on the formalities of traditional geometrics. Ann would then
adapt Doreen's finished piece to her style, free-wheeling with a rotary cutter
and a machine-driven needle. When Ann was taken ill suddenly, Doreen took
the altered piece back and added some udders. The result is *Co(w)llaboration.*

Although collaborative quiltmaking goes back to the earliest American
quilts, a new form is currently popular in the quilt world. Groups piece or
appliqué center blocks and ask friends to add borders of their own design in
trades called Round Robins. But few friends work so differently as do Ann
and Doreen, and even fewer find the level of trust that allowed Doreen to
hand over a finished top to a woman with a rotary cutter in hand.

This piece says a lot about their friendship, and it also has something to say
about the machine in terms of both function and freedom. Because Doreen's
top was machine-pieced, Ann could cut across the seams and reassemble it.
Had Doreen stitched it by hand, the seams would have raveled. But more
important is the attitude that Doreen describes in relation to her own work.
"If I don't have to commit a year and a half to a quilt I'll take more risk. I'd
be less likely to be innovative without the machine."

PLATE 49. FLY AWAY,
made by Jacquelyn Hughes Mooney, San Diego, California, 1996.
58 x 82 inches.
Machine-pieced and machine-quilted.
Collection of the maker.

Quilts share much with other art forms. They are about color, pattern and line, shape and texture. But they are also about fabric. Quilters view the world as an enormous treasure trove of found objects, all demanding to be used. Jacquelyn Hughes Mooney's quilts capture that delight in fabric and pattern. The sewing machine allows her a freedom of expression, a quickness in setting down her ideas that handwork would inhibit. "So much fabric; so little time."

PLATE 50. JANE,
made by Jacquelyn Hughes Mooney, San Diego, California, 1996.
65 x 60 inches.
Machine-pieced and machine-quilted.
Collection of the maker.

It may be that the world is divided into two types: the precision quiltmaker
and the impulsive quiltmaker. Jacquelyn Hughes Mooney's quilts have the
freshness and spontaneity that characterize the artist who works as she plans.
Certainly handworkers can be spontaneous, but the speed and the efficiency
of the sewing machine adds a level to that kind of impulsive production. "I
always tell people that the reason people in the past sewed by hand was
because the machine hadn't been invented yet," she says.

PLATE 51. STAR CHAIN,
made by Harriet Hargrave, Arvada, Colorado, 1982.
68 x 68 inches.
Machine-pieced and machine-quilted.
Collection of the maker.

Harriet Hargrave used a traditional color scheme, repeat and pattern to give her machine-made quilt the appearance of an antique. For this piece she developed techniques to mimic the denseness and detail of old-fashioned hand quilting, taking machine quilting beyond the merely functional grid or repetative jig pattern. Hargrave's work has been extremely influential in changing the way we quilt and appliqué. She has revised her popular manual *Heirloom Machine Quilting* three times. One version or another sits next to many a quilter's machine.

Plate 52. Blue Medallion,

made by Harriet Hargrave, Arvada, Colorado, 1984.
68 x 84 inches.
Machine-pieced and machine-quilted.
Collection of the maker.

Harriet Hargrave advocates using the sewing machine to obtain hand-quilted effects. This quilt is an excellent example of her mock hand-quilting. With its framed format, effective use of striped fabrics and intense quilting, the design is typical of the early 1980s, when, inspired by hand-sewer Jinny Beyer, quilters rediscovered pre-Civil-War medallion quilts. Harriet's quilt is the machine stitcher's version, proof, as she says, that machine quilting is "an art . . . just as is hand quilting. The needle just moves faster!"

PLATE 53. SCRAPPY SAWTOOTH,

made by Carolyn Miller, McKinney, Texas, 1997.
98 x 89 inches.
Machine-pieced and machine-quilted.
Collection of the maker.

Carolyn Miller is one of Harriet Hargrave's students. She combines a love for antique quilts with a mastery of her machine to create new quilts in the spirit of the old. She copied this quilt from an antique in her collection, using new fabrics that mimic the look of the naturally dyed cottons from the mid-nineteenth century. Machine piecers are reveling in the traditional patterns composed of right triangles like this Sawtooth. Speed cutting and stitching methods for triangles are creating a revival of interest in such designs.

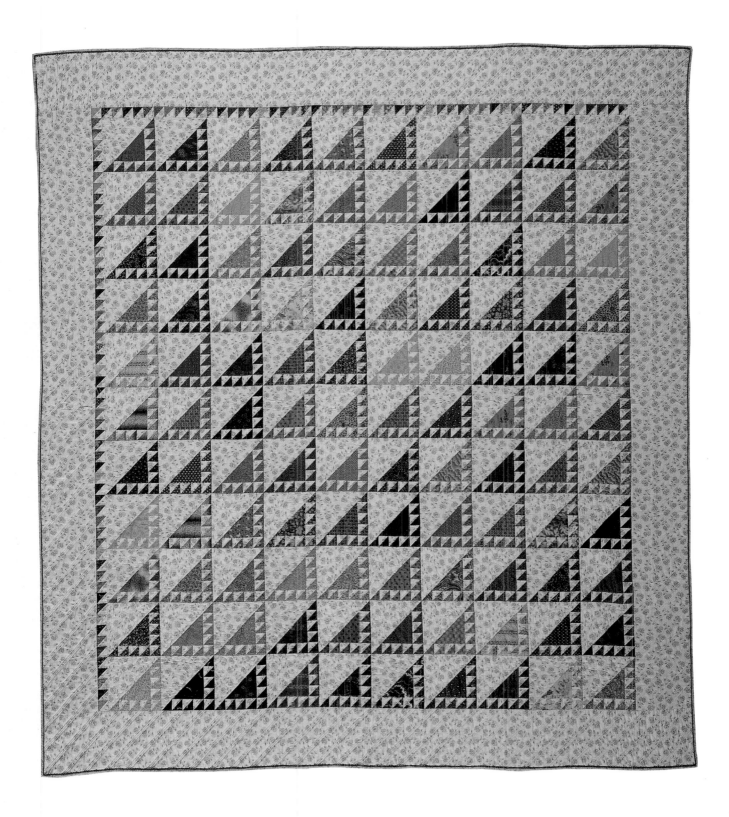

PLATE 54. MOUNTAIN SPLENDOR,
made by Carolyn Miller, McKinney, Texas, 1996.
93 x 93 inches.
Machine-pieced, machine-appliquéd and machine-quilted.
Collection of the maker.

Mountain Splendor is a version of a traditional design called *Delectable Mountains*, a name evoking an allegory from that staple of the nineteenth-century home library, *Pilgrim's Progress* by John Bunyan. Carolyn has added a leaf and vine border, machine appliquéd with Harriet Hargrave's methods of mock hand appliqué. This very traditional design stitched with up-to-the minute tools and techniques can stand up against the masterpieces of the last century.

PLATE 55. ME AND MY 404 BLUES,
made by Caryl Bryer Fallert, Oswego, Illinois, 1987.
52 x 52 inches.
Hand-dyed, printed and discharged fabrics, machine-pieced and machine-quilted.
Collection of the maker.

Caryl made this quilt for a contest called "A Palette of Prisms," in Cazenovia, New York. The challenge was to work in twelve shades of one color. She won first prize with her self-portrait at her sewing machine. The piece is two-sided, with a patchwork back of traditional quilt blocks, her tribute to the many anonymous quilt arists of the past.

Art Center College of Design
Library
1700 Lida Street
Pasadena, Calif. 91103

PLATE 56. NECTAR COLLECTOR,
made by Caryl Bryer Fallert, Oswego, Illinois, 1994.
59 x 73 inches.
Hand-painted and machine-quilted.
Collection of the maker.

Caryl works in series. This is fourth in a series of painted whole-cloth quilts. She painted the fabric with fiber reactive dyes and then layered it and quilted it by machine. She describes the machine quilting as a "major design element in this piece, providing a foreground dimension that is contrapuntal to the painted background design. Top stitching thread in many different colors was used, so that the stitching could be clearly seen against the background . . . . With the exception of the hummingbird, all of the machine quilting was done free hand, i.e., without marking the quilt top, or following a pencil line. The sewing machine needle is my drawing tool, and I draw with thread directly on the quilt as it is being quilted."

PLATE 57. JOURNEY II,
made by Erika Carter, Bellevue, Washington, 1995.
50 x 46 inches.
Hand-painted, machine-appliquéd and machine-quilted.
Collection of the maker.

In this series Erika addresses boundaries and definitions of self, the spiritual journey referred to in the title and alluded to in the imagery of the rectangular pathway. Both technique and imagery are metaphorical in her quilts; the quilting echoes the construction of the quilt and its meaning.

The hard edge of the machine-quilted line contrasts with the softness of the raw edges of the fabric, creating the tension she seeks in her work. When she wants a different aesthetic, Erika hand quilts, playing with the dimpled look of the broken line that hand sewing produces.

PLATE 58. INTERIORS,
made by Erika Carter, Bellevue, Washington, 1996.
46 x 67 1/2 inches.
Hand-painted, machine-appliquéd and machine-quilted.
Collection of the maker.

Erika has machine-quilted a gridded pattern in the outside edges of this piece, alluding to the traditional and functional quilt as covering, but she has not measured the grid. She uses a small stitch, bypassing the feed dogs that mechanically pull the fabric through the machine needle. Stitching in this fashion reveals all the starts and stops and other irregularities. Her unmeasured line and irregular stitch reveal the hand of the artist who is guiding the cloth under a mechanical needle.

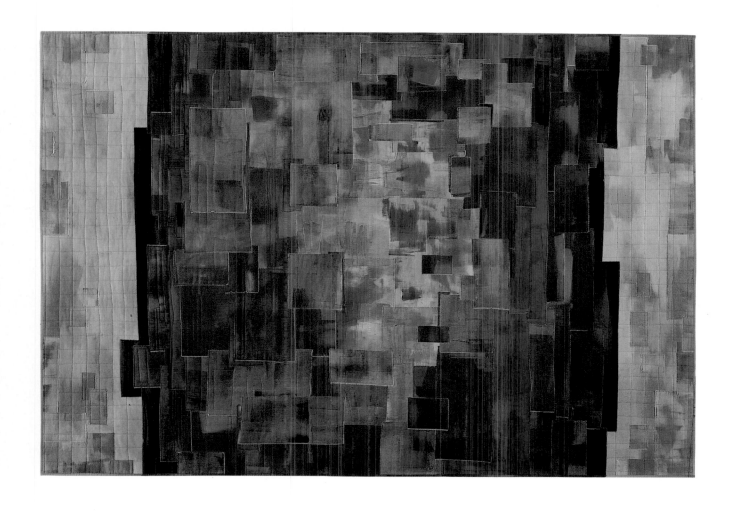

PLATE 59. LIFE ON THREE LEVELS,
made by Therese May, San Jose, California, 1995.
66 x 67 inches.
Hand-painted, machine-pieced, machine-appliquéd and machine-quilted.
Collection of the maker.

Few quilters flaunt the machine stitch with Therese May's exuberance.
She was among the first to so freely adapt the form and the techniques of the
quilt. Quilts like this horrified traditionalists, who measured the worth of a
quilt by the neatness of its stitches. But May's spontaneity, humor and freshness
gave new direction to those who valued innovation and expression.

PLATE 60. QUILT CONVERSATIONS,
made by Therese May, San Jose, California, 1990, 1996.
64 x 64 inches.
Hand-painted, machine-pieced, machine-appliquéd and machine-quilted.
Collection of the maker.

Echoes of tradition reverberate in this piece as Therese incorporates patchwork standards such as the medallion set with borders framing a central design. Images and shapes repeat to create pattern in fabric and patchwork. Yet the surface, the imagery and the energy are non-traditional, completely Therese's own.

PLATE 61. VIREYA,
made by Ruth Powers, Carbondale, Kansas, 1996.
68 x 56 inches.
Machine-appliquéd, machine-embroidered and machine-quilted.
Collection of the maker.

Ruth says she prefers handwork to sewing by machine, but this quilt was made to beat a contest deadline, so she made the most of her time by stitching the piece on the machine. Her feelings about the sewing machine summarize those of many other quilters. "Handwork is relaxing. Machine quilting is work." *Vireya* won second place in the floral theme category at the American Quilters' Society show in 1996, competing against quilts done by hand.

Quilters have embroidered the surface for centuries, adding line and images with needle and thread. New machines and new machine techniques allow texture and detail that used to take years by hand.

PLATE 62. JOY RIDE,
made by Libby Lehman, Houston, Texas, 1996.
80 x 80 inches.
Machine-pieced, machine-appliquéd, machine-embroidered, and machine-quilted.
Collection of the maker.

The square on point, the center diamond, is a standard of traditional quilt design, especially among the Amish people of Lancaster County, Pennsylvania. Amish design, ideas and color schemes have had a profound impact on mainstream quilters over the past twenty years. Libby Lehman's center diamond quilt explores the layers of traditional design, while adding a new surface with her machine embroidery.

PLATE 63. AFTERSHOCKS,
made by Libby Lehman, Houston, Texas, 1992.
50 x 30 inches.
Machine-pieced, machine-appliquéd, machine-embroidered and machine-quilted.
Collection of the maker.

In *Aftershocks*, Libby Lehman has shattered the traditional design format of the quilt, fracturing blocks and borders and adding an overlay of machine-embroidery that adds to the explosive energy.

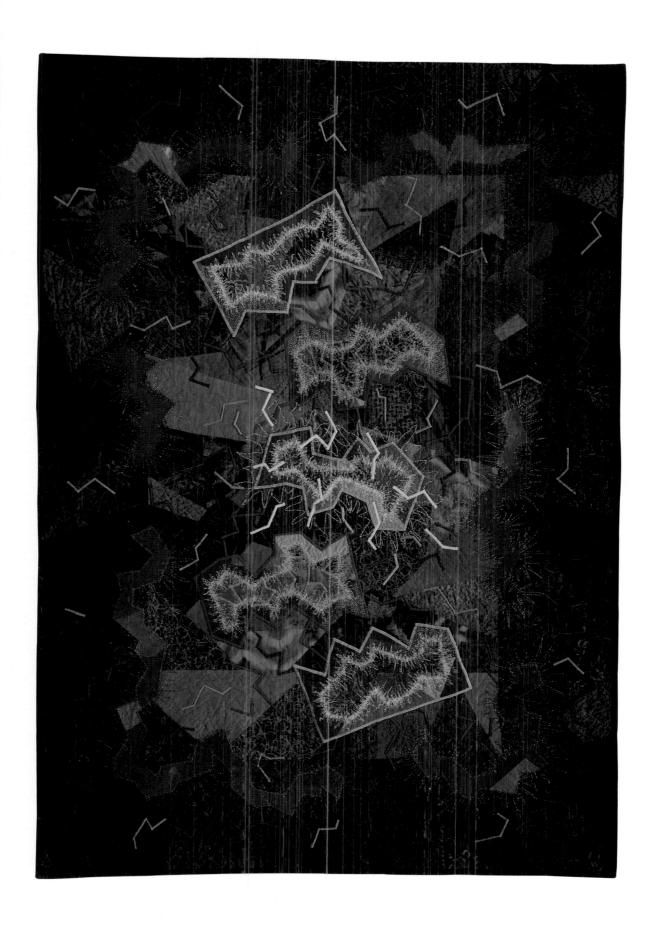

PLATE 64. NAT LOVE AFRICAN AMERICAN COWBOY,

made by Carolyn Mazloomi, Cincinnati, Ohio, 1996.
60 x 72 inches.
Hand- and machine-appliquéd and machine-quilted.
Collection of the maker.

Carolyn Mazloomi is working on a series of quilts inspired by African-American cowboys. Nat Love drove cattle in the heyday of the big herds, and was one of several men who claimed the nickname Deadwood Dick. His memoirs of his cowboy days and rodeo successes added to the mythic stories of the West. Carolyn's portraits combine hand and machine methods. She chooses the tool most practical for the image she is trying to create.

PLATE 65. DELTA BOUND,
made by Miriam Nathan-Roberts, Kensington, California, 1992.
67 1/2 x 67 1/2 inches.
Hand-dyed, machine-pieced, machine-quilted.
Collection of the maker.

Miriam Nathan-Roberts's quilts create a wonderful tension between what they look like and what they actually are. She loves to contrast metallic shades and shapes with the soft surface. Her quilts, stitched with virtuosity on the machine, can be seen as the metaphor reflecting the contemporary quilt—women working with a traditional handmade form in the midst of the machine age.

PLATE 66. FIBER DANCE,
made by Miriam Nathan-Roberts, Kensington, California, 1996.
61 x 57 inches.
Hand-painted, machine-appliquéd, machine-quilted.
Collection of the maker.

Fiber Dance is one of a recent series by Miriam Nathan-Roberts. These quilts intrigue the viewer for many reasons—the rather mysterious hand-painted surface of the fabrics, her signature tension between image and materials. But for those who make quilts, the question is always—how does she do it? Quiltmakers spend a good deal of their time trying to persuade a material with soft, draping qualities to lie flat within a series of ninety degree angles. Some are more successful than others.

How *does* she do it? She draws a full-size design, cuts the individual paper pieces out, dyes and paints the fabric for each piece, stabilizes the fabric with an iron-on backing and machine-appliqués the pieces in place. Miriam challenges herself to a formidable design of curves and angles, proving she is a master of the raw materials and her major tool—the sewing machine.

Art Center College of Design
Library
1700 Lida Street
Pasadena, Calif. 91103